THE HORSE IS MY TEACHER

Lessons from the Ranch: Training, Riding, Luck, and Love

VAN HARGIS

Foreword by Laura McClellan

TRAFALGAR SQUARE
North Pomfret, Vermont

First published in 2022 by
Trafalgar Square Books
North Pomfret, Vermont 05053

Disclaimer of Liability
The author and publisher shall have neither liability nor responsibility to any person or entity with respect to any loss or damage caused or alleged to be caused directly or indirectly by the information contained in this book. While the book is as accurate as the author can make it, there may be errors, omissions, and inaccuracies.

Trafalgar Square Books encourages the use of approved safety helmets in all equestrian sports and activities.

Library of Congress Cataloging-in-Publication Data
Names: Hargis, Van, author.
Title: The horse is my teacher : lessons from the ranch: training, riding, luck and love / Van Hargis.
Description: North Pomfret, Vermont : Trafalgar Square Books, 2021. |
Summary: "Stories from a rural working life that teach us how to be better horsemen-and better people. Van Hargis grew up in the saddle on an East Texas ranch, training his first horse at age 12 and eventually making a living starting cutting and reining colts, many of which would leave his hands to become champions. Naturally outgoing (labeled a "talker" by teachers in grade school), Hargis shared stories and lessons from his work with horses early on. Here, in his first book, he reaches out to readers with a collection of down-to-earth, highly relatable tales-experiences that, over the years, have impacted his own horsemanship and life in significant ways. Readers absorb fundamental knowledge of horses skillfully embedded in genuine anecdotes straight off the ranch"-- Provided by publisher.
Identifiers: LCCN 2021012147 (print) | LCCN 2021012148 (ebook) | ISBN 9781646011810 (paperback) | ISBN 9781570769917 (epub)
Subjects: LCSH: Hargis, Van. | Horsemanship--Texas, East. | Cowboys--Texas, East--Biography. | Texas, East--Biography. | LCGFT: Autobiographies.
Classification: LCC SF309 .H364 2021 (print) | LCC SF309 (ebook) | DDC 798.2092 [B]--dc23
LC record available at https://lccn.loc.gov/2021012147
LC ebook record available at https://lccn.loc.gov/2021012148

All photographs courtesy of the author unless otherwise noted.
Book design by Ellie Woznica, Woznica Book Design
Cover design by RM Didier
Typefaces: Carta Marina, Adobe Garamond Pro,

Printed in the United States of America
10 9 8 7 6 5 4 3 2 1

DEDICATION

Perhaps typical of a Texas southern gentleman cowboy, I of course
dedicate *The Horse Is My Teacher* to my momma, Miss Carolyn Sue Stockton.

Mother and I have been through hell on earth together. We made that journey over
twelve long years. If there's any way that a mother and her only surviving child can get
any closer, twelve years of surviving harsh lies and severe physical and emotional abuse will
surely cinch one up closer to the other. During that difficult time in our lives, I'm certain
that for Mother, I was her hope, and for me, she was my rock. Although while in the
presence of our abuser we both lived in fear most of the time, we seemed to find
comfort in knowing we were as strong as could be when we were together.

During those years of my childhood, I never questioned my mother's love and
commitment to me. I've learned to appreciate how hard she must have worked to
create any sense of normalcy in our all-but-normal home life. In retrospect, I know now
how incredibly difficult and challenging that time of mother's life must have been for her.
There was the loss of my older brother James Allen, in a tragic car accident, followed soon
after by a divorce from my father. Then she faced the reality of raising, caring for, and
providing for a dangerously curious and rambunctious three-year-old momma's boy
(that'd be me). At first when Mother married my stepfather, we were both elated.
He seemed perfect—he had a cool car, cool horses, cool parents (which meant
I had another set of cool grandparents). It seemed like an exciting new start.
Mother did not know that the years that were to follow would forever
change the core of who she was and would become.

What I learned from Momma during that time was her undeniable love
and commitment to me as her son. She committed herself selflessly to my
development. She insisted I be mannerly and respectful. She made sure I had every
opportunity that we could remotely afford, even if it meant she had to hide such things
from my stepfather. After Mother decided that we had been on the hell trail for far too
long, she mustered up the courage and bravery to leave him, keeping her
plan a secret from me until the morning of our escape.

Relief! Freedom! Yes, we felt both of these things…in part. But now Mother
faced the reality of raising, caring for, and providing for a dangerously curious and
rambunctious now-sixteen-year-old momma's boy with an insatiable appetite. Even though
I had worked to save money enough to buy my own truck and contributed all I could from
jobs hauling hay, working cows, and riding horses, my mother still worked three jobs at
times. She worked a full-time job for a company from which she would later retire after
approximately forty years. She also worked at the nearby Braum's, cooking hamburgers and
dipping ice cream. (She'll tell you to this day that dipping hard frozen ice cream was the most
physically demanding job she's ever had.) And she poured drinks at a club in a neighboring
town on any night other than those nights I played a game for one of my sports teams.

Mother served on the Commerce High School Athletic Booster Club. I'm
reasonably certain that every parent of a child that played any sport for Commerce
High School knew my mother. Certainly, all my teammates knew "Mama Sue," as
they nicknamed her. In all my years of participating in Little League baseball and basketball,
then all the junior high and high school sports of football, basketball, baseball, and track,
my mother never missed a game or a meet. There were times when the only adults
supporting our team during out-of-town games were the coaches, bus driver, and my mother.
If my teammates were not sitting on the bench or on the field or infield, rest assured they
were in the stands, sitting and cheering with Mama Sue. Even when I went to college
Mother attended all my college football games—home and away—save one. The year
we played Eastern New Mexico State University in Portales, New Mexico, she could
not find a ride and didn't trust her car to make the thousand-mile round trip.
For the first time in my life, she missed seeing one of my sporting events in person…
and I scared her to death. The second play of the final quarter, I got injured for
the first time in my entire athletic career. Mother had to follow along with
the sports commentary on the radio, and as mothers do, assume the worst.
I was fine. It was nothing a surgery, a cast, six weeks of rest,
and a few months of rehabilitation wouldn't heal.

Years later I learned that my mother was the best darned grandmother that
two girls could have. By this time my career as a professional horseman was flourishing
and required countless hours of work on the ranch in preparing horses and myself for
competition. Weekends often meant a great deal of travel. For every moment I
was not available for my girls, my mother was there for them.

Never, in any situation have I ever felt that my mother was anything but supportive
of anything and everything I chose to do in life. She certainly did not always agree with me,
but she demonstrated support, nonetheless. I cannot begin to tell you how knowing that no
matter what happens in one's life, there's at least one fan on earth that will be there in your
stands, corner, or arena…no matter what the circumstances. For me that person
was and is my mother, Mama Sue, Miss Carolyn Sue Stockton.

CONTENTS

Special Thanks

To the teachers, coaches, councilors, and pastors that have influenced and guided me—thank you. To the cowboys, trainers, and horsemen that have shared their experiences, suggestions, and wisdom—thank you. To every horse, even the Palomino filly I never succeeded in riding—thank you. In one way or another I have learned lesson after lesson from the countless horses that I have been blessed to work with throughout my decades as a horseman. I'm grateful for each one.

Without a doubt this book would have not been written if it were not for a few key and influential people in my life. Giving gratitude as well as credit where credit is due is of great importance to me; however, the number of folks that have influenced me would truly be too many to list, and I'm certain I'd fail to list them all. Therefore, I'm going to express my appreciation to a few that were more directly involved with this book's production. First of all, I must acknowledge my wife, Miss Melanie Marie Hargis, who has been the greatest supporter and motivator and most patient partner in all we've done together since she rescued me on a fateful night from "The Pigeon Lady." I cannot begin to express enough gratitude to Miss Laura McClellan who began to inspire me soon after we met. Her tenacity and drive to keep moving forward is truly amazing. Nothing I can do, say, or write could begin to do justice to her ability to overcome. It was Laura who first said to me, "You should get serious about writing and sharing your story." Heck, she helped me realize I had a story to tell.

A most sincere thanks to two of my favorite and influential teachers, Ms. Ruth Ann Coffey and Ms. Janet Peek. You'll read more about them in the chapters that follow. They both contributed immensely to my self-confidence at critical times during my teenage years at Commerce High School.

Thanks indeed to Sonny Long, who I first met while he was a writer for *The Advocate* newspaper in Victoria, Texas, when he approached me about doing a story about me. Sonny was gracious enough to listen to my stories, record them with a voice recorder, and later transcribe them, making it easier for me to eventually write them out. Thanks to Miss Emily Haun, a former student of my Top Hand Horsemanship Academy. She not only heard and learned from most, if not all, of the stories in this book, but she also assisted in correcting spelling and punctuation in the early stages of editing prior to submitting to the publisher. Which brings me to my final special thanks in regards to *The Horse Is My Teacher*: I'd like to extend thanks to Miss Rebecca Didier of Trafalgar Square Books for giving me the opportunity to submit this book concept and patiently guiding me and encouraging me to see the project through to the end.

FOREWORD

I FIRST MET Van Hargis over thirteen years ago. My family had just moved from Washington State and had bought a small acreage in rural northeast Texas. For the first time in my adult life, I was able to indulge a childhood dream: to have my own horses living on my own property, where I could see them in the pasture from my kitchen window.

One of the three horses we brought with us from Washington was a young, untrained palomino Paint mare named Angel. She was intended to be my husband Mike's horse, but first we had to make sure she was safe for a novice rider. I was tasked with finding a trainer somewhere near our new home.

One afternoon I was flipping through my new issue of *Horse & Rider* magazine and started reading an article that quoted several horsemanship professionals. One of them, I discovered, was based in Sulphur Springs, Texas—less than half an hour from our farm. I emailed the man by the name of Van Hargis to ask whether he was accepting any new horses for training. At his invitation, we drove up to meet him at his ranch, and after one conversation, we signed up immediately to have him train Angel. As we drove home after that first meeting, Mike and I both marveled at not only how knowledgeable Van was about horses, but about his skill at communicating what he knew in a way that made it easy for us greenhorns to understand.

Over the years that followed, we got to know Van as he trained Angel, and then a young Arabian mare I bought for myself, and then a young rescue colt we were fostering—but even more importantly, as he taught *us*. Week after week he shared with us the things we needed to know to be better riders and to better understand what our horses needed from us.

Here's what I know about Van Hargis: first, you won't find a better horseman anywhere, and second, he's that rare creature—a master horseman who's also a master communicator. He's a man who has spent a lifetime observing horses and the people who ride them, thinking deeply about what he's observed, applying to his own life lessons the horses have taught him, then sharing those lessons with horse lovers around the world.

That's what this book is about. I first heard most of these stories from Van's own lips during the hours I spent in his arena and in a chair outside his barn. It's been obvious to me since I first met him that Van's truest passion and his greatest gift are in teaching the rest of us what horses have taught him. If you ever get the chance to see him in action, at a clinic or horse expo or some other venue where he's demonstrating his skill with horses and his gift of teaching humans, I urge you to grab the opportunity to see for yourself what I mean. In the meantime, I hope you'll savor the lessons he shares in *The Horse Is My Teacher*.

Laura McClellan
Royse City, Texas

PREFACE

SINCE MY EARLY experiences with horses, folks have frequently said that I have a way with them. Although I don't give much merit to the comments, I understand people most likely intend them to be complimentary. I appreciate it. When people get a little better grasp as to what I do with horses, they say things such as, "You must really love horses." Honestly, I think to myself, *Yes, I do*, but not likely in the sense or to the degree they're probably thinking.

When I think of someone truly "loving horses," I tend to think of the starstruck horse-obsessed young girls that darn near eat, sleep, and dream about horses. You see, I was raised with horses. They were a huge part of my family's livelihood—a means to our survival and a major part of our cowboy-ranching culture. Additionally, I was an only child; therefore, our horses and other livestock were my friends and playmates. So, do I love horses? Yes, but again, not like some would think…and certainly not like I did as a child. Today, when I hear, "You must really love horses," I immediately think, *Yes*, and respond with a more accurate statement such as, "I love people. I love helping people. I love the horse and I'm grateful for the horse because the horse has been the vehicle that has made it possible for me to do what I truly love, and that is to help people."

Because of what I have learned about horsemanship over my more than half-century of existence so far is that problematic issues people experience with their horses reveal a great deal about themselves—their character, their habits, their focus, the way they think about problems and solutions. Years ago, in the very early 2000s, I quite by accident and by the grace of God spurted out and coined the phrase, "Horsemanship is an opportunity to practice 'humanship.'" Yes, I love horses because they have time and time again bridged the gap from where I am to where I want to be as a man. I love horses because they brought into my life either directly or indirectly the most influential people of my time on this earth, men and women who greatly impacted both my personal horsemanship and "humanship"—folks like Jack Brainard, Tom Dorrance, Ray Hunt, Buster Welch, Leaton Ely, Lynn Palm, and more. These are but a few who greatly influenced my horsemanship, and as my horsemanship improved, so did my "humanship." As my "humanship" improved, so did the opportunity to use both the horsemanship and "humanship" to help people. We might be discussing horses and learning horsemanship, but those incredibly valuable lessons were and are life lessons.

Recently, at a ranch horse clinic in central Texas, three other horsemen and I were addressing the large group of attendees. While doing so I mentioned the name Tom Dorrance. It was apparent by the blank gaze back from the audience that they did not know who I was referring to. So, I asked, "How many of you have heard of Tom Dorrance?" No one raised a hand. "How many of you have heard of Ray Hunt?" Again, no one raised their hands. "How many of you have heard of Jack Brainard?" A few raised their hands at the last, probably because it happened to be a stock horse event associated with an organization that Jack Brainard played a major role in founding.

The other three clinicians and I looked at each other in absolute disbelief. We could not believe this group of horse folk, ranging in age from nine to well over seventy, did not know who these great influential horsemen were. I immediately felt compelled to be more vigilant in informing them and all I encountered as to who they were and the lessons they were gracious enough to share with our generation. It is imperative that those of us alive today who have been positively influenced by these horsemanship legends humbly and enthusiastically share their names with each and every person we meet on our horsemanship journey. I personally challenge other trainers and clinicians to quote them often and then reference the source of those quotes as being these influential greats of our time, lest their names be shamefully forgotten. Humbly give credit where credit is due, and mention the men and women we have all learned from with respect to all they've given us to improve both our horsemanship and "humanship" journeys.

Jack Brainard, Tom Dorrance, Ray Hunt, Buster Welch, Leaton Ely, Lynn Palm, and others would not have likely been on my life's trail had it not been for the horse.

So, do I love horses? Yes, because horses bring people into my life—most to learn from and a few to help. We are on a magnificent journey during our short lives on this God-created earth. I'm grateful and blessed every day for horses and the mentors and students they have brought into my life.

VAN HARGIS
Victoria, Texas

CHAPTER I

THE SPIRITUAL GIFT

ONE OF THE best sermons I've ever heard was delivered by Brother Kris Childress at The Gathering, our small-town church in Sulphur Springs, Texas. The sermon was simply titled, "Your Spiritual Gift," and it seemed to hold my attention more so than usual.

I'm a notetaker during most sermons, speeches, or meetings. I find this not only helps me learn in the moment, it also helps me review and refer to the context for future reference. On that day, however, I was so enthralled by Brother Kris' passionate delivery of his message, I failed to take a single note until I got home from church, when my pen rushed to scribble out the words so masterfully spoken that day, lest I forget them. Then, I pondered, *What was my spiritual gift? What was my calling? What was I truly passionate about? What was it that I'd do regardless of the income? What was it that gave me a sense of peace and purpose when I did it?*

The answer to these questions was a revelation and developed into the messages I try to convey in my clinics and podcasts, and in this book, today.

I grew up in Campbell, Texas, about an hour east-northeast of Dallas. My stepfather was a trade-school teacher in the Dallas school district. He and my mom married when I was barely four years old. Every evening when my stepdad would get home from teaching, he and I would work with horses. That was my initial exposure to horse training, and a lot of what I was taught or that I witnessed was stuff that I knew I didn't want to do. My stepfather was a very difficult man. He was an abusive man—to my mom, to me, and to the horses. I hate to say such things about someone, but it's the truth.

Many years later I'd realize that people who are hurting, hurt other people. Therefore, I suppose my stepfather was very unhappy and frustrated with his life. Perhaps something incredibly painful dwelled inside of him. Anything weaker than him usually got the brunt of his frustration and anger. Knowing what I know now, the horses he handled were horrifically abused. He was just flat-out mean to them at times. And as I got older, he was flat-out mean to me, too. Also as I got older, I became more aware of and more observant of his meanness and cruelty to my mom, physically and emotionally. For twelve long years these things played on my mind. I tried not to dwell on them. It was just part of my makeup…part of my growing up.

A number of years later, after I started my own horse training business, a friend of mine bought a mare. It wasn't a good purchase. Curt was a very green rider, but he wanted a horse. So, he went out and bought one without any advice from anyone more experienced with horses. He was very proud of himself. He called me and said, "Hey, Van, I bought this three-year-old Appaloosa mare." I asked if she was going under saddle yet, and Curt said without hesitation, "No." I then asked him why he had, first of all, bought an Appaloosa (I hope this doesn't offend any Appaloosa people), and second of all, bought a three-year-old that had never been ridden.

"You don't know how to ride that well yourself," I said.

Of course, his reply was, "That's what you're for. I'm going to send her down to you and you're going to ride her for me and get her going."

I agreed because Curt and I were friends, and maybe I also put more work on this horse than I would've for the average client. I hate to admit it, but I did. I wanted the absolute best for him. There's an old saying in the horse industry that goes, "Green on green makes black and blue." Well, here he was, as green as a gourd and the horse was too. What I wanted to do was avoid that black and blue thing, for my friend's sake.

I worked very hard on that mare and got her riding around really well. Then about three months after Curt brought her to me, he called me one evening and asked how she was doing. I told him that she was going quite nicely. "I've been riding her in the arena, out on the ranch, and down the roads," I said. "Why don't you come by one day after work and ride her"?

The very next evening Curt came by. I had his mare saddled as well as one of my own horses. Just to be on the safe side, we rode in the arena first to make sure the two of them would get along. Then I suggested that, before it got dark, we should take a ride down the road. "I want you to see how she does on a trail ride," I said. For me, because I'm always working so hard with performance horses in the arena, going out on a little joy ride with a buddy was like a mini-vacation—a relaxing treat. I was really looking forward to it.

For a while we rode along the road talking and enjoying each other's company. I was also enjoying seeing him enjoying his horse.

About thirty or forty minutes into the ride, Curt's horse started darting and weaving from one side of the road to the other. Because Curt was such a green rider, I assumed he was overriding the mare, like oversteering a car. I mentioned this, and he made an effort to relax and not be too quick to correct his horse. As I looked on, it sure seemed like Curt was doing everything correctly, but the horse was still darting and weaving around. I began to get embarrassed and frustrated because I had put a great deal of time and energy into the mare's training. I really thought she was farther along than she appeared to be. After several minutes trying to coach Curt through the situation, I finally suggested that we switch horses.

"You get on my horse, and I'll get on yours. I'll see if I can figure out what's going on," I said.

I swung up on the mare, and we rode off for a few steps, and sure enough, she started doing the same thing with me. The strange part was, she'd never done the behavior before. Even in her first few rides, she hadn't darted or weaved like she was on this ride. I just couldn't put the pieces of the puzzle together. *Why was she behaving this way?* More frustrated, I decided to speed her up and drive her body between my legs and reins to keep her straight. That was a terrible mistake. It would be years later that I would learn this valuable lesson from a mentor: "Every time you gain speed, you lose about thirty percent of the control you thought you had." I wish I had known that then.

I was headed off down the road, several yards ahead of my friend at this stage, and the mare was still trying to dart left and right. I worked hard to keep her between the reins, but she was still weaving. Well, eventually we came to a bridge. Now, I don't know how many folks have ridden horses across a bridge, but those who have will know that given the opportunity, a horse will go right down the middle of a bridge to avoid the edges. So, here's Curt's horse, still darting and weaving toward the ditches, and I thought, *Okay, I'm just going to get on the bridge, drop the reins, and she'll go right to the middle.*

We got on the bridge, I dropped the reins, and…she started drifting over toward the right edge.

My ego had been touched a bit by then, and as we got closer to the bridge railing, I thought, *Fine. I'm just going to let you go, and when you realize there's nothing down there, you'll be quite happy to get back into the middle of this darned bridge.*

The ego is a horrible thing. And I let my ego hold on a little too long for safety's sake.

As the mare drifted a little bit closer to the side of the bridge I realized, *Darn. She's going to bump the bridge railing.* I picked the reins up to guide her away from the edge, but I'd waited a fraction too late, and she bumped the bridge railing with her right front knee. The moment she hit the railing, with no hesitation whatsoever, she jumped.

Jokingly, I tell people now that if a "Whoa" and a bit could stop a horse, I could have stopped her in midair. I shouted, "WHOA!" at the top of my lungs while I pulled back on the reins with every ounce of energy I had, but it wasn't until almost fourteen feet later that we stopped. We stopped suddenly. We hit bottom. We landed on the bank of the creek. Hard.

During the very brief fall I learned that my right arm must be at least a little stronger than my left—as I futilely braced on the reins, I pulled the mare's face around slightly to her right. The brunt of all her bodyweight, plus me and the saddle, landed on the left side of her neck with her legs up the steep bank of the creek. Then we flopped violently, and with just as much sudden force, I felt water slap the left side of my face and the reality of being underwater came to me. My first thought was that the mare would roll over or slide downward farther into the creek and squash me. Instead, she didn't move a muscle. I thought the impact must have stunned her.

I began to kick her with my right leg—all her body weight was on my left leg, which was trapped between her and the mud. I kicked and kicked and kicked her with my free leg, trying to get her off me. She still didn't move a muscle. By now I was thinking, *This really isn't a good situation. I'm underwater and can't breathe.*

My mind was racing. I could actually see my black felt hat, floating on the surface of the creek just above me. The angle at which we had landed had me trapped with my seat still firmly planted in the saddle. I was not able to bend my upper body in any way to get my face above the water. I was stuck. She was not coming to. She was still not moving.

I'm not sure how much time actually went by—it seemed like several minutes passed, although I'm sure it was only fractions of seconds. I began to realize I was going to have to take a breath eventually. I was so close to the surface, yet I couldn't reach it. I just kind of relaxed. I know it sounds weird, but I was thinking I would never have guessed in a million years I would die on horseback and certainly never on horseback underwater. My next thought was, *Thank God Curt is up there on the road, and he can go tell everyone where I am.*

At the very moment I thought, *Thank God*, the mare began to struggle. As she slid down into the water with me, I could pull my left leg out some—not quite all the way, but far enough that I could twist and arch my back to get my face above water. I took the biggest breath of life you can imagine. I gasped for air and again thought, *Thank God*, all at the same time. I was so relieved. The mare struggled to get up on all four feet and staggered into the water with me as I fought to stay clear of her so as not to get stepped on or hung up in the saddle or reins. She then waded out of the water and lunged up the bank, making her way up to the road toward Curt and my horse.

I was stunned. I was grateful. I was thinking about all the things that had gone through my mind during that time underwater. People tell you that their lives pass before their eyes in such situations—well, I don't know that mine did. I will tell you this: So many things went through my mind, so quickly. As weird as it may sound, it was a very peaceful feeling. I didn't have horrible regrets, and I certainly wasn't afraid of dying.

But the entire experience was very confusing to me. Why had the mare darted and weaved? Why did she jump off the bridge? Why didn't she move after she landed at the bottom of the creek? Why didn't I drown? How did both of us walk away, unhurt? My mind wrestled with all those things as I stood there, stunned and soaked from head to toe in the creek water, my left side coated with slick, smelly mud. Eventually I recovered my floating black hat, poured the water from it, placed it back on my head, and made my way up the steep bank to where Curt was waiting with the horses.

"Are you okay?" he asked in a panic. "You're covered head to toe with mud! Are you alright?"

I was perfectly fine. Everything was fine. By this time, it was beyond dusk, nearly dark, in fact, and way past time to get back to the ranch. I suggested that he just pony his mare back from my horse, and I would walk on foot. Again, he asked if I was okay. I'm certain Curt thought my idea of walking back to the ranch in the dark was odd. I told him I was fine, but I had a lot of things to think about. Bless his heart—I'm sure Curt thought I had lost my mind because the ranch was nearly two miles away. As he rode one horse and led the other, he looked back frequently as if to ask again if I was okay. I waved him on and squished along, making my way back to the ranch, one sloppy step after another.

My life may not have flashed before my eyes while underwater, but a myriad of memories flooded through my consciousness as I sloshed my way back home. Every step of the way I thought…I thought about my mother marrying my stepfather and those twelve long years of progressive abuse. I also thought about how he exposed me to horses and how I met some tremendous people through him, because of the horses. I thought about how my mom worked so hard to get me ready for grade school. The school in Campbell where we lived was so small that it didn't have a kindergarten. Most kids in our school district went to a private kindergarten, then came back to Campbell for first grade. We didn't have the money for that. So, mom made sure I knew my A-B-Cs and 1-2-3s. She made sure I was prepared for first grade. If I had stayed in school in our small town, I would have been one of eight in my graduating class.

I thought about all those things and how important they were to me. I thought about high school and how I was blessed to have had phenomenal teachers, coaches, and the opportunity to develop my athletic skills. I had flourished in high school sports. I was good enough to earn a scholarship to college.

While in college I had no real plans. I had no idea what I wanted to study. I was just thrilled to death to be on the football team and able to go to class every day. I took courses my buddies were taking, whether in physical education or business. I had no idea what I wanted to be "when I grew up." I had no plan or direction.

Then I began to develop certain interests, and some of my professors began to develop a certain interest in me. They noticed I was doing well in marketing classes and recommended I take more of them. The same with speech courses. The people around me began to guide me and take me places I didn't even know I wanted to go.

I thought about all this, too, after almost dying in the creek under that horse.

The pieces of the puzzle began to come together for me. I remembered how I met some of my heroes in the horse business. It seemed everything had just been laid out for me. Things working out the way they did surely couldn't all be coincidences.

The more I walked, the less I squished. The more I walked, the more my past and the evening's circumstances began to make sense.

Oh, how I wish I could say that I had it all planned out from childhood that I'd grow up to be a renowned horseman and travel the world, teaching horsemanship and what I call "humanship"—that ability to ultimately help people through working with horses. I wish I could say that I knew exactly what to study and how to best prepare to be what I am today. Sadly, I cannot. I was like dust in the wind during my youth, school-age years, and early adulthood. I had no idea what was in store, nor how to prepare for it. Yes, I wish I could say I had it all planned out. The hardcore fact is…I didn't have a clue. I followed those around me and was fortunately guided by some great folks who loved and cared enough about me to encourage me to keep moving forward.

All these years later, that long, wet walk comes back to me as one of my life's most important experiences. Frequently, I refer to that moment of being dunked in the creek under that three-year-old Appaloosa mare as a second baptism. I accepted Jesus Christ in my life as my Lord and Savior when I was sixteen and thought I knew what that meant at the time. However, I really didn't grasp it until years later. And I wish I could say with all honesty that the moment I was dunked in that creek was a moment of revelation, but once again, I didn't know it at the time. It was only years later that the "Aha!" moment finally came.

Everything happens for a reason. Without a doubt, everything happens for a reason. When I began to question what the reasons were for my fall into the creek, it was then that I remembered what Brother Kris Childress shared that Sunday in his sermon entitled "The Spiritual Gift." He described a spiritual gift as one's purpose. I believe that everybody has a purpose. We may not necessarily know what the purpose is early on, but I believe part of our journey in life is discovering it. It's our own spiritual gift, and to me, that is God's way of using us to serve others.

I look back at that experience of the mare jumping off the bridge and darn near drowning me as a way that God perhaps forced me to look back at the countless situations and circumstances in my life that had been masterfully engineered to expose me to the people I needed to teach me the things I needed to learn—and ultimately help me realize my spiritual gift.

For example, I wouldn't be the horseman I am today, perhaps not even a horseman at all, if my mother hadn't married my stepfather. When I consider how abusive he was, it can be difficult to accept that he is a part of my spiritual gift. But I learned things from the experience of being raised by him. I learned the type of husband I did not want to be. I learned the type of father I did not want to be. I learned the type of man I did not want to be. I look back at him as a horse trainer and I realize, even though he meant well, he was very misguided. He also taught me the type of horseman I did not want to be.

Still, it was through him that I was exposed to the horse training world.

I met some horse trainers who taught me what to do with a horse instead of what *not* to do with a horse. As an only child in my stepfather's household, I had lots of opportunity to reflect and get to know who I really was. I learned I could have relationships with other beings—horses, dogs, cattle—and that activities with those animals could be great outlets and learning experiences. In high school, I learned how to develop the discipline to become a better student and a better athlete. To improve oneself takes discipline. When I got to college, I learned there are people you meet who care enough for you that they will guide you along the way, and if you put the next foot forward, you'll be prepared for wherever you end up. Who would have dreamed then that I would one day be self-employed? Who would have dreamed then that I would need the business skills and marketing skills to do what I do now? Who would have dreamed then that English and speech—two of the courses I disliked the most yet excelled in—were preparing me for a career where speaking, teaching, and writing would be important? I needed every one of those tools in place, and every one of those experiences, in order to one day fulfill my spiritual gift.

So, what is that spiritual gift today? People say that, because I am involved with horses, I must really love horses. I do. But, honestly, if horses were removed from my life tomorrow, it wouldn't break my heart. What *would* break my heart would be an inability to work with and help people. *That* is my spiritual gift. The horse is my vehicle to reach people. Because of the training I was blessed with as a youngster and then developed through the years, horses taught me many lessons that I can now share and use to help others. I believe that my purpose in life is to help people achieve what they want to achieve in life by using the skills and processes conducive to being successful in horsemanship. I sum that up as horsemanship being an opportunity to practice "humanship."

There is an old cliché that says something like, "The two most important days of your life are the day you are born and the day you find out why." I've also heard people say that discovering one's purpose is what life is all about. Perhaps that is true, but I'd like to think it is only part of the story. The actual application of that purpose and using that purpose productively to leave the world a better place would better define for me what life is all about. I've had students over the years ask the perfectly legitimate question, "How does one know what one's spiritual gift is?" or "How does one determine one's purpose?" Honestly, I'm not exactly sure.

For me, the discovery took God "re-baptizing" me. The day the mare jumped off that bridge and landed on me, I went into the water as one man and emerged someone different. The change was not immediate, but it was a change. My awareness of the past and present seemed heightened. I was more curiously determined to connect the dots of my past experiences. Until that time I was still struggling with what I needed to do in my life. I was certainly at a crossroads and questioning myself about my career, my ability to support my family, and the typical things young husbands and fathers stress over. I prayed for guidance, confirmation, and affirmation. The bridge incident forced me to take a realistic look at my life up to that point and what I really wanted to do going forward. The result? The discovery of my spiritual gift… my purpose—the thing I had unknowingly but willingly been prepared to do since before I could remember. The thing that, when I was doing it, seemed to stop time. The thing that gave me the greatest sense of service and achievement. The thing I'd do even if I didn't get paid a dime to do it (many times I did not). The thing that I was incredibly passionate about doing. The thing that gave my heart peace.

I cannot fairly express the relief it was to discover my spiritual gift and purpose. I'd wish such a discovery for everyone. However, please know that just because you find that thing in life you know you are supposed to do does not mean that doing it will be easy. I can't count the times I've uttered words that hinted at the intention to quit. However, I could not deny my purpose, and in a short time, I'd be right back on track.

If I could encourage everyone to do one thing, I'd encourage them to frequently ask themselves what brings them the absolute most joy in life. What are they truly passionate about? What makes their heart feel at peace? When one can combine that peace and passion in their lives, the result just might be one's spiritual gift.

"The two most important days in your life are the day you are born and the day you find out why." I can't say I can remember being born and I can't remember the exact date that the Appaloosa mare jumped off that bridge with me, but I'm so incredibly grateful for both. I'm also grateful for all the moments and countless people in between. I'm grateful for discovering that horsemanship is an opportunity to practice "humanship," and I pray that this book helps each and every person who takes the time to read it. I'm grateful for all of you…it is you who make it possible for me to do what I'm most passionate about and what brings me peace…it is you who afford me the opportunity to fulfill my purpose and realize my spiritual gift.

A footnote to this story is that the Appaloosa mare I was riding, I found out later, suffered from "night blindness"—the inability to see in low-to-no-light conditions, which can be congenital and present at birth. As we rode and dusk began to fall, she couldn't see where she was going, causing her to drift, dart, and weave. She jumped the bridge railing after bumping into it, not realizing there was nothing but space and gravity on the other side. The mare was fine after the incident, and from that day forward, only ridden in broad daylight.

CHAPTER 2

MOMMA WILL TELL YOU...
THE HORSE WILL TEACH YOU

When I was growing up in Northeast Texas' Hunt County, most of our summer evenings were spent at the main door of our horse barn, watching the horses go around and around on our homemade electric horse walker. We exercised our horses at night that time of year to avoid as much of the Texas heat as possible. We'd exercise four horses at a time on the walker, for about an hour. We ate plenty of dust, but at least the air was a bit cooler with the sun long gone for the day. When the Texas Rangers were playing baseball, we might take a small black-and-white TV to the barn with us, prop it up on a five-gallon feed bucket and watch the game while the horses worked.

This practice made for long days, as the sun did not go down until almost nine at night in midsummer. My day at the barn, preparing my horses for 4-H horse shows and rodeos, started early, and my stepfather did not get home from the Dallas Independent School District, where he worked and approximately eighty miles from our home, until well after five o'clock.

One of those evenings in 1973, a noise from the far side of the barn caught our attention. The ruckus sounded like a couple of horses were fussing with each other in one of the larger stalls. My stepfather did the usual: he told me to go see what the commotion was all about.

I was nine years old, fearful of snakes, and reluctant to venture alone into the shadows on that side of the barn. Each step I took beyond the barn light's glow was deeper into darkness. I convinced myself that my eyes would adjust to the dimming and I'd soon be able to see well enough to find out what the horses were doing that caused so much noise.

By the time I got to the area of the barn from which the noise had come though, the horses weren't making a peep. Since I was all the way over on that side of the barn, I thought I might as well look in on Missy and give her a loving rub and pat. Missy, an eight-year-old Quarter Horse mare, was just under fifteen hands, very well built, and the gentlest horse on our place. When I reached her stall, I found her standing as still and as quiet as could be, with her head in the far corner of her stall and her butt at an angle toward the door. So, I simply walked in and patted her on the rump.

KABOOM!

On my hands and knees, I crawled out of Missy's stall into the open aisle. My head felt as if it were ten times its normal size. I tried to call out for my mother but my mouth wouldn't work. I could feel my face swelling. I could see something dripping to the ground below me. I knew it had to be blood, but nothing I saw had color or texture. Everything seemed unreal. I kept trying to call out to my mother, who was on the other side of the barn, still watching the four horses on the walker. Nothing but moans would come out of me. The harder I tried to cry for help, the bigger my head felt.

Time slowed as I dragged myself from Missy's stall. Although it seemed like I had been crawling for a very long time, I had moved only just past the stall door. I was confused as to what had happened. Was it real or just a nightmare? One minute I was walking up to a horse I knew and loved, and the next nanosecond I was crawling along the floor with a head too big to lift.

As my senses started working again, I could see the color of the fluid dripping from my face and mouth. It was blood. A lot of it. I felt pain but I couldn't determine where it was coming from. I hurt all over. My head and face hurt, but so did my back and shoulders. I struggled to make a sound louder than the ringing in my ears and head. I did not know what else to do, so I kept inching toward the light I could see in one direction. If the light was heaven, then maybe there would be answers and relief. If the light came from the other side of the barn, then my mother would be there to help me. Either way, it was the direction I needed to be moving.

Thoughts rambled through my confused mind: What could have made my head so big so fast? Why couldn't I look up? Why couldn't I lift my head high enough to see where I was crawling?

Finally I heard approaching footsteps. I could tell by the footfall that it was my mom, and she was moving fast. I knew when she turned the corner, and I knew the moment she saw me. She screamed. I thought, *Oh God. How bad is it?*

As she rushed to my side, my mom cried out, "What happened?" I couldn't tell her. I tried, but still nothing would come out of my mouth except moans. She lifted me from the ground, yelling to my stepfather, "Get the truck! Van's hurt!" She ran with me in her arms toward my stepfather who had jumped up to see what she was yelling about. "Go get the damned truck!" she ordered. "Fast!"

He did. He ran past the front gate, climbed into our new '73 Chevy crew cab, and raced the truck through the gate and into the barnyard area. I could hear the walker rattle and shake, the four horses pulling back against it in four different directions as the truck hurtled toward them.

My stepfather jumped out while the truck was still rolling and ran to our side to open the rear door. Mother climbed in with me still in her arms. By now I was hurting pretty darned badly. I felt the pain even more as my stepfather slammed the truck into gear and stomped on the gas. He pulled out of the barnyard and headed for the highway without even stopping to close the front gate. I couldn't help thinking how many times I had been punished for leaving a gate open. I wondered if the front gate being left open now would be my fault.

We lived midway between Greenville and Commerce, nine miles from each. Both towns had hospitals, but the Greenville hospital was regarded as a bit better than the one in Commerce, so we turned to the right at the end of our driveway. My stepfather pushed the truck's 454 engine to its limit. We hit the interstate at record speed; it seemed like we were passing the world. Big tractor trailers seemed to be standing still. I was hurting so badly, yet all I could do was moan. I remember thinking, based on my limited experience, that my head felt like a bale of hay or a sack of feed on my shoulders. Those were the heaviest things I'd ever lifted by myself at that point in my life.

After exiting the interstate in Greenville, there were a few signal lights between the highway and the hospital, but I don't recall my stepfather stopping at any of them. He just kept his flashers on, honked the horn, and cussed like crazy as we blew through the intersections. When we arrived at the emergency room entrance, he drove the truck right up onto the sidewalk, as close as possible to the door.

I had visited this hospital several times before because of my asthma, so I was familiar with some of the staff there. My old friend, Mrs. Wilkens, met us at the emergency room door. Mrs. Wilkens was an emergency room nurse, and the sweetest and gentlest woman I knew outside of my family. She was a very tall, fair-skinned, Black lady who always made me feel comfortable. I always felt like she'd just as soon take me home and care for me as a mother would a child rather than as a nurse treating a patient.

Through the haze of my pain, I was relieved to find Mrs. Wilkens there. Being in my mother's arms and seeing Mrs. Wilkens gave me the sense that I would be okay. They had seen me through many emergency room visits before. I knew my mother and Mrs. Wilkens would get me through this one too.

Now, I don't want to sound like I was a frail child who spent most of his time going back and forth to the hospital. I just had a few allergies that caused my asthma to flare up. In fact, one of the things I was most allergic to was horses and other animal dander. The fact that I was so outdoorsy and athletic meant that at times I pushed myself and my asthma to the limits. That often resulted in a trip to the emergency room to set things straight.

X-rays, examinations, lots of stitches and bandages, and a mouth full of wire somehow put the nine-year-old Humpty-Dumpty together again. After a few visits to the oral surgeon to set and treat my broken jaws, I lived with my mouth wired shut for several weeks. I had to learn to eat, drink, and take medicine through a straw. This proved to be a very difficult task in the beginning. Unfortunately, the first pain medicine that the doctor prescribed came in the form of capsules that were, of course, too big to fit into a straw. While we could have poked the capsules through the holes where my teeth used to be, my fear of gagging on a whole capsule made it seem too dangerous to try. My mother came up with what seemed like the perfect alternative: she bought ice cream and whenever it was time for a pain pill, she made shakes for me to sip through a straw—with the medicine mixed in.

The first time Mother entered my room with a big frosty glass in hand, brimming with a chocolate milkshake with the medicine dissolved and carefully mixed in, came soon after I returned home. I was hurting pretty badly and looked forward to a little relief from the pain. And getting a whole chocolate shake would be a great bonus.

Dang, that shake tasted *bad*! I don't suppose there was enough chocolate or enough ice cream in Texas to hide the taste of those pills. I suffered through the shake ordeal for quite some time until the doctor got around to prescribing something else. (I rarely drink milkshakes today, but when I do, the first taste is still done with measured caution.)

Youngsters can be fairly resilient, and thank goodness I was. Though it seemed like an eternity at the time, I was over the ordeal with the medication in a few weeks and was quickly on my way to recovery. While I recuperated at home, mother made sure I kept up with my school work by getting my assignments from my teachers and bringing them home to me. Mother told me that the teachers all joked that now that I was all wired up, maybe I would be quiet in class. Those who've met me as an adult will not be surprised to learn that as a child, I was a talkative and social young fella. I frequently got in trouble at school when, after finishing my work in class, I left my seat to visit with the other students, and at times, even offered to help them with their assignments. Both my mother and my teachers apparently thought that having my mouth wired shut for a while might deter me from being so vocal. Their hope turned out to be misplaced—during my home convalescence, friends from school and members of our 4-H club and horse club would come visit me, and I was soon talking up a storm right through the wires on my teeth and jaw.

When I was able to go back to school, all the kids and teachers wanted to see my mouth full of wires. I had to answer a lot of questions about my jaw and how the whole situation happened. It was then that the teachers learned that having my mouth wired shut was not going to lead to the result they all hoped for. Shortly after returning to the classroom, I came home with a note from my teacher: "Even having his mouth wired shut doesn't keep this boy from talking." Not only did I learn to talk through the wires, I perfected the art.

Back in those days, our school report cards included a grade in "Deportment," a fancy label for evaluating a student's manners and behavior. On the first report card after the accident, my Deportment grade was "S-" (less than satisfactory). Under the Deportment heading, a list of subcategories identified for parents the behaviors that resulted in the student's Deportment grade. There was a subcategory labeled "Talkative." Above that word, my teacher had written in bold red ink the word "VERY." The little box beside "VERY Talkative" was marked with not one, but three check marks, also in red ink.

Perhaps being a public speaker for a living was my calling. Heck, many years later my dear sweet grandmother even said, "Van, good thing you get paid to talk, 'cause Lord knows you sure do a lot of it."

After several more visits to the oral surgeon and dentist, the day finally came to have the wires removed from my mouth. Mother asked me what solid food I wanted to eat first. Back in those days, I truly loved McDonald's Big Macs. There happened to be a McDonald's restaurant just down the street from the doctor's office. I ordered three Big Macs. I was only nine years old but was certain I could eat all three. It had been about ten weeks since I had last eaten anything solid, so I was craving those hamburgers in the worst way. Smelling them and watching as they were prepared just about made me crazy. As soon as the person behind the counter handed the tray with our food to me, I ran to the closest table and unwrapped one of the Big Macs as fast as I could while Mother followed with our drinks and napkins. The moment I had been waiting so long for had finally arrived.

Just as I was imagining what it was going to be like to taste that first bite, I realized that I couldn't do it. I wanted that burger so badly, but I simply could not get my mouth open wide enough. Because my jaw had been wired shut for so long, I needed to retrain my muscles to be coordinated to open and chew. And, after weeks of consuming only liquids, I lacked the confidence to try and bite. Something that always seemed so easy and natural suddenly was a chore to me.

By the time my mother reached the table, I had tears in my eyes. I couldn't eat a hamburger. I wondered if I would ever be able to have solid food again.

In the days that followed, mother and I worked at developing that confidence and those biting and chewing skills. We started with mashed-up bananas and gradually worked our way to foods with a bit more solid consistency. It wasn't long before I could eat small bites of some favorite foods. Mother promised that as soon as I thought I was ready, we would go back to McDonald's, and eventually I did, in fact, eat three Big Macs in one sitting—the memory of which would cause a chuckle amongst family for many years to follow.

Frequently I think about the lessons I learned from getting kicked in the face by a horse. Missy, the mare in the stall that summer night, was the gentlest and kindest horse on our ranch. In one fraction of a second, though, she taught me what my mother had told me since I was big enough to walk: "You better quit walking behind those horses or you'll get your head kicked off," and "You'd better let those horses know where you are when you're walking behind them or you'll get kicked."

I suppose all caring parents want to protect their children from what they know could hurt them. My mom was the best at warning me about the things I was about to get into. Perhaps I was stubborn or just simply the type of young fella that wasn't going to learn from a verbal or written message. It seems I learned best from experience.

Some might say that what happened to me was tragic. Some might blame the horse for kicking. Never have I ever looked at that experience as a bad one, nor did I ever blame the mare. She certainly surprised me by her reaction that night, though, and I *did* want a chance to surprise her back. An idea of how I could do that came to me while on an adventure with one of my friends, Bobby.

Like many young boys in Northeast Texas, I owned a lever-action Daisy BB gun. I'm sure you know the kind of BB gun I am referring to: the kind that you'd cock one time and it would shoot out a single BB that moved so slowly you could watch it emerge from the end of the barrel, fly through the air, and make contact with your target. I used to try to shoot birds with it, but most of the time they'd either get hit and fly away unhurt, or they'd see the darned BB coming and fly away in time to avoid contact. I'm fairly confident a BB could be thrown with more velocity than my rifle could "shoot" one.

Bobby and I were playing with our Johnny West toys out in the pasture when we decided to play a real game of "Shoot 'em up, bang-bang." Bobby hid in the tall grass, and I hid in a little washout. Once in a while, we'd poke our heads up to see where the other was, and when we did, we'd shoot our BB guns at each other. If my momma had seen this, she would have tanned me good. Likely I wouldn't have been able to sit for a week.

Nevertheless, Bobby and I, with no regard to previous parental warnings, continued to shoot our BB guns at each other until I heard, "OUCH!"

I hit him. I won.

Bobby staggered from behind the tall grass as if acting out some movie scene, his hand covering his forehead right between the eyes. Suddenly, the seriousness of the moment dawned on me. When Bobby removed his hand from his forehead, I saw the unmistakable sign of the BB's contact centered between his eyebrows. That BB left the smallest bruise I have ever seen.

There was no blood, so I was hopeful that no real damage had been done.

"I'm not hurt," Bobby insisted. "Just surprised."

Acting fast to cover up the evidence of The Gun Fight at Grass Gorge from any suspecting discipline-oriented parent (namely, my mother), I spit in my hand, rubbed it in the dirt, and commenced with smearing mud on Bobby's forehead.

I got to thinking how Missy "surprised" me that night in the stall, and now I knew how I could surprise her back.

One day when the mare was grazing close to the house, I grabbed my Daisy BB gun from my closet. "I'm going to surprise Missy, Mom!" I yelled as I headed toward the pasture.

Spying my BB gun, Mother understood what I had in mind. She followed me outside. "You aim carefully," she said, "and shoot for her butt."

Missy barely even acknowledged our approach. When I got within range, I cocked the gun, took careful aim, pulled the trigger, and watched the BB arc through the air toward its target. When it hit Missy on the rump, she raised her head, swished her tail, and looked back over her shoulder at my mother and me. I'm sure Missy wondered why we were laughing so hard. She went back to grazing, and we walked back toward the house with a certain amount of satisfaction evident in my smile and stride. Apart from the memory of having been kicked in the face and all awful the stuff that went with it, the entire event was now behind me.

For several reasons, I am fortunate to have had the kick happen so early in my life. First, at the age of nine, one heals quickly. I suffered very few long-term physical effects from that accident. Second, Missy taught me never to take a horse for granted, not even the gentlest and kindest horse on the place. That night Missy was minding her own business and likely was partially asleep in her stall. When I walked in unannounced, I surprised her, and in that moment, she simply acted like a horse instead of a babysitter for a fearless nine-year-old boy. She did what horses do, what horses have been doing for thousands of years, long before humans intervened in their lives: she protected herself. As a prey animal, one of the horse's primary defense mechanisms is a lightning-fast reaction time when danger presents itself. Unfortunately for me, a nine-year-old's head happened to be at just the right height, like a golf ball on a tee, for that mare's hoof to catch me directly in the face.

No, I don't blame Missy. In fact, I think positively of her almost on a daily basis. I am thankful for her and for the lesson she taught me about horses. Because of that lesson, learned while I was a child, as an adult I now can say honestly what few horsemen can say: I have been hurt by a horse only twice— four decades apart—in all my years of working with them. I have started under saddle thousands of horses and travel the country teaching others how to do so. Horsemanship has been my calling and my work for almost my entire life, and I am proud to say, "Thank you," to Missy for teaching me to be careful, to think ahead, and to never take situations for granted.

Oh, I also appreciate my mother for trying her dead-level best to keep that kick from ever happening. Her frequent warnings were heard loud and clear. I suppose there are times in one's life when Momma will tell you, but the horse will teach you.

CHAPTER 3

INCH BY INCH

DURING MY YOUTH it was very common for our family to gather each Sunday at my grandparents' house south of Sulphur Springs, Texas. The routine was pretty much the same for years. The usual family members at our get-togethers were: our gracious hosts and my grandparents on my mother's side of the family, Allen Ray and Della Fay Gammill, whom we all affectionately call Gaddy and Della Hay; mother's sister, Wanda and her husband, my cousins Gina and Daron; and finally, my mother and I. We all thought of my grandparents' place as "home" for various reasons. My grandparents seemed to be the strongest and most stable limbs of our branch of the family tree. My grandfather was also the oldest of his five siblings; therefore, following the death of my great-grandparents, Gaddy's house became the primary meeting place for his brother and sisters whenever they were visiting or passing through.

Though my grandfather had been ill from heart and lung disease for many years, it was obviously the highlight of his week to have the family come each weekend to visit, watch the Dallas Cowboys, or just sit around and play card games or dominoes. As with most any true-blue Texas family, the weekends during football season were reserved for the Four Fs of Texas: family, food, fun, and football. After the game we would celebrate victory—or complain about the mistakes that were made by the players, coaches, or both if the Cowboys happened to lose. Of course, if it happened to be baseball or basketball season, we'd practice the same armchair sports ritual, but with the Texas Rangers or the Dallas Mavericks, respectively.

Regardless of the season or the occasion, the best part of being at my grandparents' house was that we were certain to have some darned good cookin'. My personal favorite meal was Della Hay's southern fried chicken. Still to this day we are not sure what her secret was, but there was a touch my grandmother had with fried chicken that just can't quite be duplicated by even those with whom she shared her recipes and techniques. Both my mother and my aunt fry chicken as good as anybody, but it still isn't quite the same as Della Hay's. Perhaps it was just the fact that *she* was the one doing the cookin'. Whether my cousins and I were in the yard playing or out in the pasture re-discovering the world, we came running quickly when the women announced that it was time to eat. Typically, when we all began to gather for dinner, the adults got first choice of the prime seats around the dining room table where all the food was located. The older kids got second choice, and so on. When I was the youngest child in the family, I got the last seat…wherever there was a place to sit. At times this would be in the kitchen or in the living room at the coffee table, or sometimes at a card table, or even at the table out on the back porch. I had no complaints though. I knew I was going to be cared for and well fed. Our family was likely not that different than many southern families in that the men and the children were cared for first by the women, who did their best to make sure we all had plenty to eat and drink, and that we were as comfortable as can be.

I can remember a few times that the weather was too bad to be outside, and I had to remain indoors during the preparation of the Sunday meal. I would wander around the house and ask questions of the adults or older children. One item of decoration in my grandmother's house, for whatever reason, stirred me to ask about it frequently. It was a cross-stitched piece of folk art given to my grandmother by her sister Helen Fulton. Though it was shifted from room to room and place to place over the years in Della Hay's house it was a mainstay of decor. (Nowadays, it is proudly displayed in my office at my ranch.)

I am not sure why I was attracted to it and wanted to read it so often, but even when I was too young to read, I remember asking my aunt what it said. She of course stopped what she was doing and answered me. On another occasion I asked my mother, "Mom, what's that thing on the wall there, and what does it say?" Mother stopped what *she* was doing and read the cross-stitched words to me. I asked my grandmother on a different day, and she too would read the decoration to me. Soon I knew what it said, and I would read it aloud to myself: *Yard By Yard Life Is Hard ~ Inch By Inch It's a Cinch.*

It was the first thing I learned to read.

Early in my life the cross-stitched piece had no real meaning to me. In fact, it was a number of years before the meanings behind the words on that artwork began to reveal themselves to me. I was training a great number of horses at the time. As many young trainers do, I worked as hard and as diligently as I knew how. I followed the advice of knowledgeable horsemen who'd come before me and tried to get as much done for both the horses and their owners as possible. But I was guilty of cutting corners in an effort to ride more horses and impress customers with the progress their horses had made. It seemed that each time I tried to skip steps in a horse's training program—doing less than the necessary amount of groundwork or putting a saddle on a colt before I had made every effort to ensure that he was properly prepared or riding a horse before he was truly ready—I ended up having problems with that horse.

Each time I tried the "Yard by Yard" approach, *I* was the one that paid the consequences. The times in which I dedicated myself to applying all the steps I knew in my heart were important and necessary for establishing a solid foundation in a horse's training, and when I took the time to do those steps properly and effectively, amazingly, I had no problems with the colts. The funny thing is, I tried to skip some important fundamentals in an effort to save time and impress owners. The truth was, it always cost me in many ways. I took chances that could have injured me or the horse. I ended up having to go back and instill fundamental steps later. Most of the time, the "Yard by Yard" approach cost me both time and energy, and on at least one occasion, a prospective good customer.

As in so many situations in life, we have to look at problems in steps. It's a process I call "reducing to the ridiculous." This example hit me one time in high school. I had a math teacher at the time who frequently asked us to approach the board in front of the class to work algebra problems as the rest of the class looked on. This truly worried me, as I struggled in algebra my freshman year in high school. I was behind the rest of the students because I had recently transferred to Commerce High School from the school I'd attended for eight years in Campbell, Texas.

During my junior high years in Campbell, I was not a very attentive student, and to make matters worse, we had no full-time junior high school math teacher. Our scheduled teacher was very ill with cancer and often not at school. Our substitute teachers kept us busy by assigning massive loads of addition, subtraction, multiplication, and division. Though this busy work was easy and made for good grades in math, it did *nothing* to prepare me for the algebra that awaited in ninth grade at Commerce High. To make matters worse, after I transferred schools, my stepfather, who insisted that I prepare to become a veterinarian, made me sign up for algebra rather than pre-algebra because that would put me on schedule to take tougher math classes later in high school. Being a vet was my stepfather's dream for me—not mine—but to keep the pressure off myself at home I did as was demanded.

The textbook was like a foreign language to me. I did not have a clue as to what I was looking at when I reviewed the problems. What were all those Xs and Ys? What was the purpose of the parentheses, and why were some numbers underlined? Where were all the regular numbers and problems like those we'd done in junior high?

I was a particularly confident young man who was not typically uncomfortable in front of people, but when Mrs. Ruth Ann Coffey called my name to come to the blackboard and solve a problem, in front of God and everyone else, I knew I did not belong there. Mrs. Coffey was tall, and a little thick in her upper body with noticeably much thinner legs. Her hair was short and white. She seemed to have a bit of a scowl on her face most of the time. It was often difficult to discern her expressions. Even when she was pleased her appearance was intimidating.

As Mrs. Coffey recited the problem for me to solve, I hardly knew how to transfer what she was saying to the blackboard, let alone solve it. After struggling to get the conundrum written out correctly, I stood there and stared at the challenge for what seemed like an eternity. I could feel all the students behind me, piercing me with their eyes. I could feel some of them shaking as they tried to hold back the chuckles. Finally, I looked at Mrs. Coffey and confessed that I had no idea how to get started. I told her I did not have a clue about how to solve an algebra problem.

I'll never forget how she responded to my ignorance.

Mrs. Coffey leaned back in her squeaky teacher's chair, crossed her arms over her thick body, and with a slight attitude to her tone asked me, "Van, can you add?"

"Yes," I said.

"Can you subtract?"

"Yes."

"Can you multiply and divide?"

"Yes, ma'am," I said, somewhat timidly.

"Van Hargis, if you can add, subtract, multiply, and divide, then you can do algebra. You see, Van, algebra is nothing more than adding, subtracting, multiplying, and dividing. The parentheses and the lines simply tell you when to do the things you already know how to do. We just take the *big* problem and make it little problems. By taking care of the little problems, the big problem gets solved."

As I listened to Mrs. Coffey's words, she seemed to transform right before my eyes. I no longer saw her as a large, scowl-faced, intimidating admiral of algebra. As she spoke, I heard a caring, supportive voice coming from a peaceful, white-haired, angelic soul who seemed now to have a glow about her that resonated out toward me. She was not there to shame me; she was there to guide me. And as Mrs Coffey continued, I thought of my grandmother's cross-stitched piece of folk art.

Algebra and folk art came together metaphorically to teach me that any and all problems can be solved if we choose to take care of the *little* things that we know how to do instead of getting distracted by the big problems. Solutions to most obstacles can be found if we take them inch by inch rather than in yards. Having the foundation training to do the simple things, such as addition, subtraction, multiplication, and division, gave me the skills I needed to solve any math problem. I overlooked the importance of those skills in algebra when I focused on the larger picture.

We all have skills that we have developed or that we will develop, and by recognizing our positive attributes and using those skills in ways we understand, our larger problems become achievable. A couple of familiar sayings go something like, "One eats an elephant one bite at a time," and "The longest journey starts with a single step." Both of these support what Mrs. Coffey reinforced in her algebra class, as does that piece of cross-stitched folk art that now hangs in my office.

As a horseman and a clinician, I'm frequently asked questions about horse behavior. Too often owners are faced with issues concerning their horses and simply don't know how to solve the problems. Perhaps like me, staring at the algebra problem on the blackboard, they are focusing on the big problem rather than thinking in terms of addressing the horse's basic training or establishing a foundation in their own horsemanship.

Let's consider a common issue for many horse owners: trailer loading. Many novice horse owners will focus on the trailer and associate the horse's negative behavior with the trailer itself. Some may read up and discover that it is natural for horses to be claustrophobic. Some will even discover that the trailer restricts the horse from doing what horses do to escape scary situations—flee. This kind of information helps a novice horse owner understand a trailer loading problem, but it still doesn't get the horse in the trailer.

In teaching people about trailer loading, I simply ask some simple questions, just as Mrs. Coffey asked me when I confronted the large problem of algebra on the board in front of my class. No, I don't ask horse owners if they can add, subtract, multiply, and divide, but I do ask them if their horses are halter trained. Can your horse lead on a rope without you having to pull him around? Can you control your horse's primary body parts—nose, hips, and shoulders—with nothing more than the aid of a halter and lead line? Can you back your horse freely and willingly on the lead line? Can you lunge your horse in circles around you on the end of your lead line? Can you lead your horse through gates with no hesitation? Can you lead your horse to a small gate, stop at the opening, and then send him through the gate by himself on your command? Can you get your horse to walk over short bridges, such as those seen in trail classes? These are all skills that a horse can learn that prepare him for loading in the trailer.

Yes, horses have fear of enclosed places, but before they can face those fears, we need to give them the skills to overcome the other obstacles related to getting into a trailer. First, they must lead very well. We must be able to move their feet and major body parts easily and responsively. We can prepare them for going into an enclosure by training them to go through gates and stall doors. We can even prepare them to step up into a trailer by training them to step up on small bridges or other secure platforms. You see, by doing all these little things, we give the horse the skills to do the *big* thing. We also develop our skills in communicating to the horse what it is that we want. In this practice both the horse and the handler develop a "common language."

When all the small skills are firmly in place, all the horse still needs to learn is when and where to use those skills. *Yard by Yard Life Is Hard ~ Inch By Inch It's a Cinch*.

Many problems, both in life and in horsemanship, can be handled in this fashion. Concentrate on the little things, and the big things become achievable. It would be unfair to horse and human to ask either one to solve a problem with no applicable foundation. With a foundation, however, most things can be accomplished.

I am eternally grateful to Mrs. Ruth Ann Coffey for not humiliating me that day in her algebra class and for pointing out that I already possessed the skills to be successful in high school math. I am also thankful to my aunt, my mother, and my grandmother for taking the time to read those words of wisdom from a cross-stitched piece of folk art to me, over and over again: *Yard By Yard Life Is Hard ~ Inch By Inch It's a Cinch*.

**I dedicate this chapter to Mrs. Ruth Ann Coffey. She kindly assisted me in learning to "reduce to the ridiculous" and focus on that which I can do to find solutions.*

CHAPTER 4

Everything Comes to He Who Waits

Just before I started the third grade, my stepfather and his aunt, Fay Cooper, decided to go into the cattle business together. Miss Fay was an eccentric person, but I liked her. She frequently included me in conversations, which made me feel significant. The only thing I didn't like about her was that she was a heavy smoker. The nasty habit contradicted the idea I had at the time of what a good role model should be. The fact was, both my mother and stepfather smoked cigarettes, too. However, Miss Fay was an elementary school teacher. I knew of no other grade-school teachers who had such vices. In retrospect, I'm reasonably certain I was very naïve.

Once a quarter, we'd get together at Miss Fay's house in Cumby, Texas, and go over the details of the cattle business. At these meetings strategies were discussed and decisions were made, such as which cows to sell and which to keep, and what repairs needed to be made at the ranch and how to budget for those repairs. Even as a youngster, I was particularly interested in these discussions because it was my responsibility to feed the cattle, especially in the winter when the days were short. It was well past sundown before my stepfather got home each day. He demanded that supper be on the table and ready to eat when he walked in the door from his nearly two-hour commute from the city. This prevented my mother from being able to help me feed the cattle. Perhaps you can understand, then, why I was so interested in the number of cows that we were to winter. The number of cows determined how many bales of hay I had to load and put out each day. This task was quite the chore for anyone but especially for a kid my age. I was but nine years old the first winter of our business with Miss Fay.

The good thing about meeting at Miss Fay's house was that as my attention span waned during the adult discussions, I was allowed to wander around her old house. As I said, she was an eccentric character, and she had a lot of interesting knickknacks and trinkets on shelves, tables, and windowsills throughout her house. There was no theme or pattern to her collection. Even as a child I could see that most of her things were likely acquired quite spontaneously.

One day I went into her office and noticed a unique wooden plaque. On it was a hot and sweaty cowboy who appeared to be stretching a length of fence. He had a dialogue balloon above him that read, *Everything comes to he who waits*, and below him read, *as long as he who waits works like hell while he waits*.

I hate to admit it, but it was the second part of the quote that caught my attention. I thought to myself, *What?* Here, again, a grade-school teacher and role model to young children had the word "hell" written right there in plain site where I could read it! A cuss word! A grade-school teacher who smoked and cussed. It's not that I hadn't heard plenty of cuss words by that time in my life, but they certainly hadn't come from the mouths of my teachers.

Well, I always remembered that darned quote, despite not having a clue as to its meaning at the time I found it. Perhaps because of the shock factor.

You never know where lessons will come from or what environment you'll be in when something is said or done that is stored in our memories. It's kind of scary, too, when you think of how we might be doing something casually or nonchalantly without giving a thought to how it might be influencing someone around us, perhaps not at that moment but maybe down the road. We need to be keenly aware of our speech and actions around others. When working with my horsemanship and humanship students, I remind them that if they're riding or working a horse—or heck, doing anything at all for that matter—and there's anyone around, anyone at all, they should be keenly aware of their actions, the things they do, and even the way they do them. We cannot escape the responsibility of ambassadorship. This is especially true when one is doing something others may look upon with favor, such as riding a horse. I always remind my students that if they are riding a horse in any public setting, or even in a rural area visible by passersby, they must be aware that someone may be watching. And because they are doing something that someone might wish to do, they are people of influence at that moment and an ambassador for good horsemanship.

So do what you do, the best you can do it, at all times. Even if you're casually riding. Casually ride *correctly*, and practice good habits. This is not only to keep you safe but to make sure you are a positive influence if someone is watching. Be a good ambassador.

I think of Miss Fay often, and I'm thankful I got something positive out of being around her and working cattle with her. The combination of her career as a teacher and her vices made her, and the quote in her office, all the more memorable.

Everything comes to he who waits…

At first folks hear this or see this and the word "waits" jumps out at them and they think, of course, about patience. We've all had people in our lives tell us to be patient. Heck, I can't count the times I've heard people say that if you train horses, you must be patient.

Yes, perhaps this does refer to being patient. Question is…patient for what? This is the important part. For what and why are you being patient? Well, the quote clearly tells you in the very first word: Be patient for "everything." *Everything?* Really? Because "everything" is so vague and all-encompassing, we move on to a word that is not so vague: "waits." We know exactly what that means, don't we? But, in fact, it is the vague word that is the word of importance. Why? Because it is so vague it can be *your* word. It is your blank space to fill in. This quote, then, can have a general meaning for everyone but mean something specific to each individual.

I can think of no better way to learn the full meaning of this quote than through horsemanship. How so? Well, many people don't realize that when working with horses, you just don't flip a switch and suddenly everything is okay. There is a tremendous amount of work that goes into working with an animal. And then there's that lesson of patience. We have to realize that horses have no concept of "time" the way we do. I joke at my clinics that I've yet to see a horse with a Timex. Yes, they know when regular feeding time is—the sun's going down, the temperature is dropping—that kind of thing, but they have no concept of the hour of the day or how long something might be taking. So if we, for example, are late getting a horse to the vet, we're not going to be able to hurry him onto the trailer because of that. Knowing that "time" means nothing to horses is a great lesson for humans. We put a great emphasis on time.

Working with horses has helped me somewhat discount time. But a struggle remains. For example, while doing clinics, I usually have time constraints. Sometimes it's not realistic to get a horse where you want him to be in his training in the number of minutes allotted by the exposition administration. Consider a horse that's never had a halter on. It's not likely you're going to get him through elementary school, junior high, and graduated from high school (in other words, gentled, saddled, and ridden) in an hour. That doesn't mean you can't be efficient with the use of your time and teach the horse and the audience as much as you can during the time afforded.

Now comes the hard work aspect of the quote—the part with the cuss word for emphasis. While working with horses, one must put in the time, due diligence, and effort to get various lessons across to the horse. To this end, there are four questions I apply to horsemanship that are applicable to everyday life as well.

- First and foremost is, "What do you want?" It sounds like a very easy question, doesn't it? Sometimes, getting specific about it, though, isn't. We must identify what we want and be as specific with that answer as possible.

- The second question is, "Is what you want fair and achievable now?" We have to be fair with ourselves and with our horses. Ask yourself if it is fair to the horse, at this point in time, given his training, ability, breed, and whatever else, to ask him to do what we want?

- The third question puts the burden back on us. "Can we communicate what we want in a way that is understood?" I might want the horse to do a flying lead change. (Question One.) Can he do a flying lead change? Is it fair to ask it of him? (Question Two.) Yes—I see him out in the pasture doing it all the time. But can we ask him in a way that he understands what we want and when we want it? (Question Three.)

- We must consider the first three questions, and then we need to ask, "How do we measure the result?" Was it a success? If not, why not? How can we go back and improve those first three processes to ensure that the last one—the measurement—is on the increase?

These questions go through my mind thousands of times when I'm working with a horse. The process they offer is a valid one and something we can use in our everyday lives. Back to that original quote: *Everything comes to he who waits…as long as he who waits works like hell while he waits*. It's a constant reminder that anything I want my horse to accomplish, whether it's being halter trained or winning the next cutting championship, means I must put the *work* in. I must *work* to answer the four questions honestly: What do I want? Is it fair? Can I communicate it? (This might be the toughest aspect as very little communication between horse and human is verbal—it's physical and visual. We have to put in the *work* and time to create a language that the horse can understand.) And lastly, we must *work* diligently to measure the results.

When I think back to that quote, I think what a blessing it was to be allowed to wander around Miss Fay's house and stumble across that darn cuss word on that plaque and learn…

Everything comes to he who waits…so long as he who waits works like hell while he waits.

CHAPTER 5

HE WHO WAITS THE LONGEST IS THE LEADER

PEOPLE WHO LOSE patience or faith in what they are trying to accomplish with a horse may hear me tell them, "He who waits the longest is the leader." If this quote and the quote from the previous chapter sound mighty similar, please know that it is by design. Both quotes send a message about patience, work ethic, and faith. Little in life is achieved without work, and in both quotes "work" and "wait" might be one and the same.

In four-plus decades as a professional horseman, I've noticed the most desired thing people want from their horses is a good relationship. A good human-horse relationship is very similar to that of a human/human relationship. A good relationship with a horse (or a human) certainly requires a lot of work and wait. It also takes work and understanding. Heck, I suppose we could just sum it all up as work. Why? True understanding requires us to objectively study and learn as much as possible about the individual with whom we wish to establish a relationship. That's not easy. It requires work.

Though, in my opinion, we could never know *everything* there is to know about horses and the lessons they have to teach us, there are a couple of key things that we *do* know about horses that can help us start to develop a relationship with them: As most of us know, they are *herd animals* and they are *prey animals*.

Let's first explore the *herd* concept. A horse doesn't care if it's you, another horse, a pony, a dog, or a goat, they are willing to "herd-up" with anything that may increase their odds of survival. We call it *herd mentality*. Horses are social animals for at least a few reasons. The first and most obvious is perhaps a bit selfish: there's safety in numbers. ("If there's two of us there's a fifty-fifty chance of survival in case of predator attack.") Another reason is perhaps a bit *more* selfish: the sharing of parasites or pests. ("If I stand really close to you, then perhaps some of the flies that are on me will go to you.") And another may be a little *less* selfish: convenience. ("If we stand side by side, head to tail, I'll swish my tail to keep flies off your face if you'll swat flies off my face.")

Whenever a human and horse are involved with one another, the relationship is a herd relationship, although horses cannot understand "relationship" from our perspective. Just as they cannot relate to our ideas of time and materialism, they are not affected by human emotions like anger and resentment. The burden is on us to understand "relationship" from their simple point of view and emulate it as closely as we can.

In the beginning of this human-horse relationship, it is imperative that we are willing to work hard to deliberately communicate in a way the horse understands. In time, as trust and understanding develop, then refinement of communication may transpire. That's what my horsemanship training program is all about: keep it simple, keep it basic, and train from the horse's perspective.

If you really want something in life that involves another or others, then it is imperative you make an effort to realize the perspective and perception of the other or others. The author and motivational speaker Zig Ziglar said, "The key to getting what you want is to help others get what they want." That's great advice in general, and it's certainly applicable when working with horses. Therefore, while working with them we should at all times consider those four questions of successful horsemanship I talked about in the last chapter (see p. 34). Additionally, we must be fully aware of *what horses want*, and that is to survive the moment with peace, harmony, balance, and efficiency. (Of course, stallions and mares are genetically programmed to continue the species; therefore, it's instinctual for them to procreate, but even with the distraction of hormones, they still desire to survive as efficiently as possible.)

Now, because horses are *prey* animals, they naturally learn from *pressure* and *release*. But what do these terms really mean?

Pressure is merely an action that threatens or implies a threat to a horse's comfort (peace, harmony, balance, and efficiency). For example, we know that horses are prey animals with big bodies and small fuel tanks. In other words, they are grazers with small stomachs and fast metabolisms and need to continually eat in order to keep their bodies fueled to efficiently escape danger. After all, their first survival instinct is to flee when something threatens their comfort. Therefore, one form of pressure could be to simply get a horse to move his feet, which consumes calories (needed to flee), which programs his brain to start seeking ways to *stop* his feet again and conserve energy.

The knowledge that a horse wants and needs to be a very efficient conserver of energy is powerful for us humans and would-be horse trainers. In order to get a behavior or a response from a horse that *we* want, we must first know what *the horse* wants. Which is easy. He wants nothing, and a lot of it. So, in order for us to get what *we* want, we may need the horse to consume energy. While he is consuming energy, we wait for him to give us an effort toward that which we want. When that happens, we immediately give him what *he* wants. Which, again, is to be efficient and conserve energy.

This is where a relationship starts and where leadership can begin. The relationship is going to be a working herd partnership between the horse and human. Controlling movement (consuming or conserving energy) will be its simple form of communication. Why? It's the kind of relationship and communication the horse already understands. It's the way horses get along with each other. However, in this relationship, someone must be the leader. Which one, horse or human? It needs to be the one that makes the best decisions on behalf of the other and for the sake of a better working partnership. The one that is perceived to control survival (peace, harmony, balance, and efficiency) will be the leader. The one that is most trustworthy and consistent will be the leader.

Numerous times I've said the best thing we can do for the horse is study the horse. Learn to know the horse for what he is: a horse. To know the horse is to know that he is a very simple animal with little to no built-in complexity—at least that's the case in a wild or more natural environment. However, to help us all get along in the domestic world, it is imperative that we work to understand the horse and all his basic needs and wants. The more we know about the horse, the more likely it is that we can provide those basic needs and wants. In doing so, we begin to understand things from the horse's perspective. It is then that we can learn to balance and obtain that which *we* want with that which *the horse* wants. Once those things are realized and understood, then a great journey together begins.

Too frequently it is seen that someone desiring to own a horse is unprepared. The person may, for example, have the means and financial resources but lack enough understanding of the horse. The responsibility of horsemanship goes far beyond that of what many folks think. In all fairness, most realize that owning a horse is challenging financially. Most know it takes a significant amount of property to house one. Most are even aware of the physical work involved with care and training. Where the horse/human relationship is usually strained is by the lack of real knowledge about the simple basic needs of the horse that I've already mentioned. We must provide peace, harmony, balance, and efficiency (survival) for the horse. The question is, how do we do that? We must know our role. In the domestic world in which we have our horses, *we* must be the leaders. We must continually demonstrate our ability to balance that which we want with that which the horse wants.

Remember the fourth question from the last chapter (see p. 35)? How do we measure the result when we ask the horse to do something we want? This is where *He who waits the longest is the leader* comes in. We have to have faith in the outcome. We must humbly know that perfection is unobtainable on this earth. We as humans and horsemen will never be perfect, nor will our horses be perfect. However, it's a great goal to strive for. In working with our horses our goals should be to always have a happier, safer, and better horse partner. In order to achieve that, we must truly work on our own skills as necessary to *always be better than we are right now.* Set long-term realistic goals. Then set short-term realistic goals. Establish a step-by-step process that will enable you to make progress toward those goals. Finally, do something! Take action of some sort. Follow the four questions of successful horsemanship and know, without a doubt, that you'll eventually achieve your goal.

For many, getting started and having faith in the outcome is difficult; it takes time and effort. That is part of the *work* and the *wait*. Waiting while doing nothing productive all too frequently results in a nothing outcome. However, waiting while working and constantly objectively adjusting and refining all those things necessary to be better yields great results. Now, that doesn't mean just "be busy." Don't do things just to do things and expect positive results. For example, if a teacher in a particular class gives you an assignment to "read the book," and you get very busy reading "a book," you could claim that you were busy working. You were reading a book. But the teacher said to read *the* book—the book relative to the class that teacher was teaching. Yup, you were busy. You were even busy reading. Yet you were busy doing nothing productive toward the assignment because you didn't read the assigned book.

It is likely we can all think of folks we know or have known that frequently seem to be busy but at the end of the day, have little accomplished. We want to work and be busy *being productive* while waiting for the outcome of our goals.

Have faith and know that your goals will be achieved. Consider, for a moment, and as we have before, loading a horse in a trailer. We've all either experienced or witnessed a horse having difficulty loading into a trailer, which is why I often use it as an example. Needless to say, it can be challenging and stressful for both horse and handler. Have you ever heard someone say something like, "I hope my horse loads today"? Apart from in religion and spiritualism, I'm not a fan of the word "hope." I'm particularly not a fan of "hope" in most horsemanship situations. Why? "Hope" implies it might not happen. I prefer the word "faith." Why? "Faith" implies it *will* happen. However, there is a missing component. *When.* When will it happen? My answer? I don't know. The preparedness of the horse prior to loading in the trailer (as we discussed in chapter 4) may determine when. My ability to communicate via a process in which the horse understands calmly and quietly may determine when. It will happen when it happens, and "it'll take the time it takes," but there's one certainty: I have faith the horse will load on the trailer. I will be more patient and persistent than the horse. I will work harder and wait longer than the horse. Why? In the domestic world the horse needs me to be the leader. A leader determines a goal, determines a plan, takes action, humbly makes adjustments or refinements while keeping the goal in mind, and has faith in the outcome. *He who waits the longest is the leader.*

Starting in my later years of high school I began to read the Bible more, as well as motivational materials and books. Amazingly, throughout the Bible and in practically every "success" book I read, there were numerous similar themes related to leadership. And amazingly, as I began training horses many years later, I noticed that as I adhered to the process of leadership (goal, plan, action, refinement, and outcome) and the guideposts I had acquired from my youthful reading, the results were quite successful. My conclusion was that horses truly needed a leader, and the fact that I had at least a proven process to follow, that perhaps helped me be more confident and deliberate in my actions, encouraged the horses to feel more confident in me as that leader. In the meantime, I worked diligently to learn more and more about horses from those who had a great deal more experience than me. And ultimately, I learned that constantly refining the understanding and the process would bring me more and more success.

Later, still quite by accident, I learned that horsemanship was a great way to practice being a leader of people as well.

In the very early 2000s I was performing horsemanship demonstrations in Mitchell, South Dakota, at a farm and ranch exposition on behalf of a sponsor. After one of the presentations, a studious-looking young lady approached me with a notepad and pen in one hand while gripping a mini-recorder in the other.

"Mr. Hargis, excuse me," she said. "I'm with the local newspaper here in Mitchell, and I was hoping I could have a bit of your time to ask about your programs."

Of course, I agreed.

The reporter went on to say that she had visited my website and noticed on the front page that it said, "Van Hargis: The Horseman with a Message."

Immediately I was impressed that she had already done a bit of research, and I quickly and proudly responded, "Yes, ma'am."

She then replied, "So, what's your message?"

Honestly, I was stumped! You see, since the late nineties I had placed that tag line, "The Horseman with a Message," on my website. It was suggested to me by a wonderful lady in Houston, Texas that had hired me to speak and perform horsemanship demonstrations. She liked the way I taught horsemanship through the use of stories and analogies and told me she was going to always refer to me as "The Horseman with a Message." I thought it sounded great and aligned with my style of teaching, so the tag line became part of my branding.

Only one problem. I didn't really have a message. I'd never given it a thought.

With a recorder stuck in my face in South Dakota and an ambitious young reporter waiting for an answer, I amazingly—or better yet, *miraculously*—told the woman that in all these years no one had ever asked me that question, and then, without a second's hesitation, I looked right at her and said as if it had been said by me a thousand times, "My message is that horsemanship is an opportunity to practice 'humanship' every day."

Shocked by what had just flowed from my mouth as if I had a prepared statement, I asked the reporter, "Did your recorder get that?" She checked and sure enough, there was the sentence playing back, "Horsemanship is an opportunity to practice 'humanship' every day."

Perhaps she saw my surprise on my face, because she asked if everything was okay.

"Yes ma'am," I said. "It's just that I've never said that before, and I'm amazed those words came out of my mouth."

The point here is that practicing good leadership skills with horses is great practice for leadership skills with humans. It takes a lot of practice; it takes a lot of work. The practice and the work is what to do while one is waiting for the outcome…and then you have to have faith in the outcome—the end goal. The one who practices the most and works the hardest is most likely to produce the greatest results. Producers of great results often earn the respect of those around them. Whether it's one horse successfully leading a herd over challenging terrain to find good grazing and water, or an athlete that always seems to be at the right place at the right time to find a way to pull out a victory in a team event, it is usually not a coincidence that these individuals are the leaders. They have survived the tough moments, practiced the longest, and worked the hardest… and *He who waits the longest is the leader.*

CHAPTER 6

WHERE YOU RELEASE IS WHAT YOU TEACH

SEVERAL YEARS AGO, I was asked by the Idaho Horse Council to be a presenter at the Idaho Horse Exposition. Occasionally at the horse expos or horse fairs, I get the opportunity to listen and watch other trainers and presenters. In one presentation at the Idaho Horse Fair, a trainer was working with a troubled horse that would not allow people to use electric clippers to trim the hair around her ears and bridle path. The trainer was prepared to show the audience how this could be achieved quietly, calmly, and without restraint or sedation.

When he turned the clippers on and the mare heard the quiet buzzing of the electric motor and clipper blades, she abruptly and fearfully moved away from the trainer and the sound. The trainer quietly and calmly maintained control of the mare and simply moved with her as she tried to distance herself from the annoying buzzing noise. He did not try to prevent her reaction or restrain her, he merely kept her from completely bolting away. The very moment the mare stopped trying to move away, or even acted as if she was *about* to stop moving, he turned the clippers off and reached up and gently rubbed the mare with his hand. The behavior he wanted from the mare was for her to stay put and relax, so he rewarded that behavior. When he turned on the clippers and she reacted by moving or flinching, the clippers would remain on. As the mare again regained her composure, the clippers were turned off.

In the beginning the mare could not stand still, but gradually she learned to remain calm as the trainer moved closer and closer with the clippers on. In time, trust was gained and empowerment was established. The horse learned to trust that the clippers were not going to harm her and the trainer was not going to force them on her. The mare also learned to control her own emotions and physical response. She learned that she was *empowered.* How? She had a wee bit of control of the situation. Her behavior determined if the clippers approached or not, and that they did so at a pace she was comfortable with.

In short, the trainer was rewarding the behavior he desired by removing pressure. He repeated this practice several times and got to the point where he could turn on the clippers and the mare wouldn't move a muscle. He could turn them on and lean toward her and get the clippers within six or eight inches. When she showed signs of being a little worried, he'd stop at that exact point and wait for her to regain her composure, once again trusting him and the clippers at the new (closer) distance. When she calmed, he'd turn off the clippers and move away from her. He persisted in this way until eventually he touched the mare with the clippers. She heard their sound and felt their vibration as they made contact with her body, yet now, she did not try to flee. And when she relaxed, he moved them away from her.

"Where you release is what you teach," the clinician told the audience. That was his lesson. I am sure everyone else thought the same thing I did: *Where you release? What?* Of course, the answer is *where you release the pressure* is what you teach the horse.

Let me explain.

Here's what I want people to realize about pressure: Pressure is perceived. It's not always something physical. At that demonstration, it was not the fact that the clippers were touching the mare or cutting her hair that had her scared. It was just the presence and the sound of the clippers that pressured the mare into a reaction (she distanced herself from the clippers, moving to an area of the ring she perceived as safer and less threatening). Too often, when a horse behaves in an unexpected or undesired way, people will say, "Well, I wasn't doing anything to the horse." *It doesn't really matter.* Sometimes it's your mere presence that's the source of pressure. Sometimes you don't have to "do" anything. Remember, its the horse's *perception* of danger or safety that determines his reaction or response.

So, I've coined an addition to go with the lesson the trainer shared with the audience that day: There is *applied* pressure and *implied* pressure. There was no physical pressure applied to the mare, but there was implied pressure when he was "in the room" with her and turned the clippers on. The clinician didn't physically touch her with them. He didn't chase her with them. He didn't do anything to her—but there was an implied pressure. He could tell that was the only amount of pressure the mare could take. Anything more than that and she would have given him more adverse behavior instead of positive behavior. And then, *the very second* he got something positive, the trainer turned the clippers off. "Where you release [the pressure, whether applied or implied] is what you teach." *What you teach* depends on what sort of behavior you want. In this case, he wanted the horse to stand still and be clipped. So he made it a step-by-step process, pairing the release with the mare standing still, and then gradually, allowing the clippers to come into contact with her body. By the time the whole process was over, he had her bridle path (the space between her ears) and the excess hair from both ears trimmed. The horse was calm and relaxed. It all took less than an hour.

I thought, *That sure beats tying them down, putting a twitch on them, sedating them, and forcing them to be clipped.* Not that I believed in using any of those methods, but that's what a lot of people would resort to instead of taking the time to teach the horse with the release.

I think about that long-ago clinic a lot and use the trainer's quote with students and guests at the ranch daily. That demonstration, and his constant use of the quote every step of the way, nailed that "plaque" to my brain's wall. I began to share the idea with people, encouraging an awareness of pressure, and teaching that when you got a behavior that you were looking for, to simply *release* that pressure. We must realize that in the horse's world, it's all about pressure or the release of pressure. Either there is peace, harmony, balance, and efficiency for them, or there's a reason for them to move their feet and consume energy and calories to avoid pressure—and seek peace, harmony, balance, and efficiency again. Our reward for them is, when we take that pressure away and give them a moment of peace, harmony, balance, and efficiency. Horses aren't greedy animals. Sometimes just a moment to experience that which they seek is all they need to get the message.

I also tell people to *just let go and empower the horse*. Reverse the table. Allow the horse to be the trainer. What I mean by that is—and I know it's kind of contradictory to what I said in chapter 5 about "he who waits the longest is the leader"—I want to empower the horse to the point to where his job is to train me to leave him alone. Whenever he's doing what I need or want him to do, I simply leave him alone. Whenever he's doing what I don't like, I present some sort of pressure to him. The minute I get what I want, I release that pressure.

This is a pretty good lesson for us to use in our human interactions, too. I've been very blessed with two beautiful daughters (now adults) who were easy kids to raise (thankfully). As the girls were growing up, folks frequently commented on their good manners and behavior. To this day, people comment on how the girls turned out to be such nice young ladies. Certainly, I cannot take all the credit, but I can't help but think of that trainer's quote, its spirit and intent, and my practice of it. I have no doubt that it influenced my approach to fatherhood and my daughters' character development. I gave my girls enough latitude to make mistakes. If they did something and it didn't go well, I'd "go Dr. Phil" on them, cross my arms, and say, "Well, how'd that work out for you?" Then I might guide them back on path. (There's the pressure.) The moment they were back on path, I "let them go," so to speak. This was a great lesson for me, too. Sometimes the hardest thing to do is not micromanage somebody or something. Put them back on path, then let them go. Imply or apply pressure as needed, then release it. Their job, meanwhile, was to train me to quit putting them back on path. After a while, my daughters began to recognize the path of least resistance and learn what their boundaries were, and therefore, what was acceptable behavior.

As parents, as co-workers, as partners in relationships, we have to realize those around us have their own individual personalities, their own desires. We have to accept the fact that *they are who they are*. As long as everyone is working within certain boundaries, we're going to get along. That is one of the things I learned from watching, learning, applying, and practicing the spirit and intent behind the lesson I learned that day in Idaho: not just putting the pressure on, but also to be willing to take that pressure off. One must have the courage to sit back and let a horse or a child be, empower them, give them the opportunity to discover their own boundaries. That's *part* of the story. The other part is that we need to be self-disciplined enough to accept a "try," accept an effort, accept who they are, accept the things in life that they can do. When I use the word "accept," I'm not talking about making excuses, such as, "Well, you know that kid—he's the troublemaker in the family." That's not the kind of acceptance I'm referring to here. In some cases, that's a copout. What I am addressing is that we must nurture a reasonable amount of acceptance, as long as it fits within our household boundaries, family boundaries, and maybe societal boundaries.

There's a story about my oldest daughter, Jazmin, that goes along with this. As I said, the girls were easy to raise. We had little regimens for them when they were young. I was the one who usually gave them their baths, put them in bed, and sang them a song at night. I'm a horrible singer, but thank God my kids were tolerant (or didn't know any better).

One night I went to Jazmin's room, and very typically, she had her toys out on the floor and was playing, but it was bath- and bedtime. While standing in her doorway, I told Jazmin to put away her toys and get ready for her bath. All of a sudden, she collapsed on the floor and threw the biggest fit. I mean one of those fits where she was face down on the carpet, fussing, kicking, and whining. Even though I was shocked by her behavior because she had never done such a thing before, I just leaned against the door and let her do it. I waited until the fit had eased, and she looked up at me. I told her again in a calm cool tone to put her toys away and get ready for her bath. Again, she did the belly roll, kicking-and-whining fit. Again, I didn't move a muscle.

By this time, Jazmin had gotten her mother's attention—her mother came storming across the house, demanding what on earth was going on. I told her that I assumed Jazmin didn't want to put her toys away and get ready for her bath. She suggested that I snatch Jaz up and give her a spanking.

"Why?" I said. "She's punishing herself."

I told Jaz a third time what needed to happen, never changing my tone. I think by then she realized I wasn't going to yield and her behavior was getting her nowhere. She finally put her toys away and made her way to the bathroom for her bath. By the time she got in bed and I started singing to her, she was as happy as a lark.

So, when people ask me how my girls turned out so well, I just say I trained them like I do my horses. I don't think the girls appreciate me saying that though.

1. My grandparents, Allen and Della Gammill, with their daughters Carolyn Sue (my mom, standing) and Wanda Lou (on the bike) in the late 1940s.

2. One of my first rides. I was two years old and held on by my granddad ("Gaddy") and my older brother James Allen, who died in a car accident shortly after this photo was taken.

3. No more than four years old, riding Flicka. ᵛ⁄

4. Reluctantly sitting on a yearling stud colt named "Cutter," son of World Champion Cutter Bill, when I was four. My stepfather is holding the colt. ᵛ⁄

5. Riding "Priss" at my step-grandparents' farm when I was around five years old.

6, 7, & 8. Showing off my 4-H horsemanship skills with an orphaned calf in the summer of 1970.

9. With my mom at Christmas in the late sixties.

10 & 11. I bottle-fed and trained everything on the ranch—from leading to riding.

12. The first thing I learned to read—a cross-stitched piece of folk art gifted to my grandmother Della Hay from her sister Helen. Little did I know this needlework would be applicable and impactful throughout my life. Today it hangs quite visibly in my office at the ranch. 🐂

13 & 14. Practicing with Priss (above) and Honey (below) before my first 4-H horse show in the early seventies. ᚼ

15. My Western Pleasure class at that first show. I'm on Honey in the center, to the left of the girl in pink.

16 & 17. Standing proudly with Priss and Honey, then displaying my winnings from the show: First place in Showmanship and Halter with Honey and first place in Reining with Priss, plus numerous other placings in Western Pleasure, Trail, Barrels, and Poles, and the High Point Award. 🐂

18. "Look, Mom. No hands!" Junior Pee Wee Rodeo in the early 1970s.

19. Our dog Monique enjoying a ride with me on one of my stepfather's customer's horses.

20. At fifteen, riding my stepdad's stud horse while ponying his roping horse after football practice. No matter how late in the day, ranch chores still needed to get done. ⅌

21. Practicing roping on "Scooby" in 1979. ⅌

22. Mr. Leaton Ely started working with me at calf-roping well before my pre-teens. Throughout my career, I continued to ride with and work with Leaton. He was one of the best horsemen I've ever been blessed to know and ride with. He was also a cowboy in every sense of the word. I never saw Leaton get in the way of his horse, and he taught me to get out of the way of mine.

23 & 24. Running for the goal line for Austin College in 1981, and determined to score at the National Championship game. ᚷ

25. In 1983 I was part of the East Texas State University Lone Star Conference Championship team.

26. Riding "Beau" while living in New Zealand.

27. My precious happy girls—Jazmin Bree (left) and Britni Skye (right). I hope they learned half as much from me as I learned from them.

CHAPTER 7

THE PATH OF LEAST RESISTANCE

THE END OF summer and early fall was always an exciting season for those of us in the cattle business. It was time to gather cattle, and sort off the calves and haul them to market. For Mother and me, it was both joyful and stressful. You might say it was a love-hate type of deal for us. We loved it because when we got our calves to market and sold, we had some money in the bank. Most of the year it seemed we barely scratched out a living. After we sold our calves, we had a little relief from our financial stresses and were able to purchase things that extended beyond the bare necessities. (For me it usually meant I'd get a new pair of boots and perhaps some school clothes. Mom might get something nice for the house. She rarely bought much for herself in those days.)

The part we hated about the cattle work was the fear and stress related to gathering, penning, sorting, loading, and hauling the cattle to market with my stepfather. As I've said before, he was a pretty hard character. He was also extremely frugal and would not hire outside help when we worked cattle. He wanted no one on the ranch other than himself, my mom, and me. It wasn't until years later that I reckoned the reason for this was because he was insecure in his abilities and didn't want other cowboys to witness his lack of knowledge about cattle and their management or his impatience and violent temper. It was easy and possibly strategic for him to isolate us and isolate himself by not having anyone else around.

After we gathered the cattle, drove them toward the corrals, and got them penned, it was time to sort the calves off their mommas and eventually load them onto trailers and haul them to market. None of these steps were easy with our sparse three-person crew. With all due respect to my mother for being a part of the potentially dangerous tasks, she was still the least experienced and least knowledgeable about livestock. Unfortunately, it was her job to work the sorting gate. During this process my stepfather and I would ease the cattle toward Mother, and we would communicate to her to let a particular animal out of the corral or keep it in. Mom needed to open and close the corral gate in perfect timing with the approaching cattle so the sorted stock would see the opening to freedom and go through or see a closed gate, which meant no escape.

It wasn't uncommon for our cattle to get a bit snorty, run at us, charge us, and occasionally try to headbutt us during this process. Like most Texas cattle raisers, we had a mixed herd. We had a registered Brangus bull and a few purebred Brangus cows, but most were crossbred cows "with a little ear," as we'd say, which meant they had a little Brahman blood flowing through their veins. This, of course, was visibly evident because their ears were a little longer than other breeds. Well, our mixed cattle could be as cool as cucumbers, or when rushed around a bit too much, could turn darned near rank. I had been taught to stay calm and deliberate in my actions, and then the cattle would usually stay quieter, too. Cattle, like most animals, sense the "spirit and intent" of those around them. They could read my stepfather, for sure. His presence alone would often make both cattle and horses tense.

The cattle could also sense my mother's mood. She was nervous and unsure of herself and the cattle, and she was certainly concerned about being yelled at by my stepfather. Picking up on mother's lack of confidence, the cattle would get a little ornery with her. Then, she would get worried and frightened, which affected how well she could work the sorting gate. Because Mom was a bit fearful, the safest place for her was at the sorting gate. It's not that the sorting gate was a good place to be for someone afraid of cattle, it was just a better place. At least at the sorting gate the fence and the gate offered a little protection.

Occasionally a cow charged at Mother and she'd simply forget her responsibility to work the gate and "miss" the cow, meaning she might close the gate on a cow we wanted out or open the gate and release a cow we wanted to keep.

Knowing this, one might begin to understand the stress involved with this task. Not only could the cattle be dangerous, if a cow was "missed," it was correct to assume my stepfather was going to be quite angry and start yelling and cussing.

(I never thought of my mother as a weak link in our little cattle-working crew, but obviously the cattle and my stepfather did.)

Even though I got no joy out of seeing my mother frightened of the cows and being yelled at, I couldn't help but enjoy her expressions and comments as she darted and jumped around when the cows got a little too close and too fast for her comfort. On one occasion, I'm quite certain I witnessed a move that far exceeded feats capable of the best of athletes. We had one cow that was particularly snorty in our herd, appropriately named Wildflower. Oddly enough, her momma was one of the calmest and quietest cows in our herd, and our Brangus bull was as laid back as a bull could be. Nonetheless, Wildflower was the complete opposite. She was as nervous as a cat in a room full of rockin' chairs. Within minutes of being trapped in a corral she would start panicking and "huntin' the gate." If you didn't get her sorted out of the pens fairly early, she'd start chasing anything that moved on two legs. I simply learned not to get Wildflower's attention when she began getting snorty. Mother, on the other hand, couldn't control her anxious emotions and movements, and the cow would charge, with Mom sometimes just barely escaping getting freight-trained by an eleven-hundred-pound scared and pissed-off cow.

Well…on this one occasion, Mom got turned around and confused about something near the sorting gate, and she moved excessively enough to get Wildflower's attention. Sure enough, the cow got Mother in her sights and charged with reckless abandon. As I watched the scenario unfold, I noticed my mom hadn't acknowledged that Wildflower was charging at her and yelled, "Mother, heads up!" Mom turned quickly toward me and saw that Wildflower was practically right on top of her and closing the remaining gap quickly with her head lowered. Mom had one hand on the six-foot board-and-cattle-panel fence, and with a blood curdling scream and a giant leap, she miraculously cleared the fence, landing safely on the other side, totally unharmed. I was amazed at what I had just witnessed! My nonathletic mother had just cleared a six-foot fence with the aid of just one hand at its top rail. Amazing! Oh, but the miracle didn't stop there. We were all astonished to see that my mother landed—get this—in an empty open-topped, fifty-five-gallon barrel that had been placed there as a trash container. Yup! A miracle? It was to me.... Hallelujah! (We needed another miracle to get her *out* of the barrel. I'll let your imaginations envision it.)

Many years later I shared the story of Mom's logic- and gravity-defying leap and landing with an artist friend. He painted a watercolor illustration that depicted mean cows running at a female figure (meant to be my mom) and escaping the corral. Under the drawing he included the caption: "Cattle are like water and electricity. They all take the path of least resistance." I never thought of my mom as a weak character, but from a cow's point of view, I reckon she *was* the path of least resistance.

After I'd hung my shingle out, announcing to the world that I was open for business as an aspiring young professional horseman, I was frequently—heck, almost constantly—reminded that horses were like cattle. They, too, seek the path of least resistance. "The path of least resistance" has since become the absolute foundation of my horsemanship program.

Long before a human ever comes into play in a horse's life, the horse naturally seeks and takes the path of least resistance. It's in his DNA to do so. Like all grazing animals of prey, horses have great big bodies with little bitty fuel tanks. Which is really just a comical way of saying they have fast metabolisms so that they can have quick energy readily available if the need to escape danger or harm arises. As we have already discussed, given a clear choice, a horse will choose the most efficient way of doing something in an effort to conserve the greatest amount of energy. This behavior becomes tainted a bit in strict domestic environments, but it is still instinctual to horses. Therefore, it is wise when training a horse to do so with these natural instincts in consideration.

Whenever I'm working with a horse, I often associate another quote with this idea of "the path of least resistance." It is, *Make the right thing easy and the wrong thing difficult*, and it has been around for decades. I'm reasonably certain that Tom Dorrance first came up with the quote and later Ray Hunt popularized it. Ray was one of the first horsemanship clinicians that traveled the country and helped people with their horse problems (and helped horses with their people problems).

I don't think Ray's quote really sank in rock solid in my mind until I tied it to my friend's watercolor illustration about cattle, like water and electricity, choosing the path of least resistance. I now look at whatever it is that I want the horse to do in this way. With everything in our horse's training, we need to think far enough ahead about what it is we want from the horse, then work to create that path of least resistance to achieve the task. Sometimes the situation is more obvious than people think. I often use the simple example of asking a horse to move to the left. The first thing many people think of or do is pull on the horse or force him. But if, instead, we "open the gate," creating an easy way for the horse to move left because there's "an opening" for him to go through, then we are offering to make the right thing easy. If the horse goes through the "open gate," great! If he doesn't, then we can add a little pressure.

When people watch me on horseback, sometimes they say, "My goodness, we never even saw you move! We never saw you kick, spur, or pull on the reins! How did you get your horse to lope around so nicely?"

All I did was refine the communication with the horse to a point that I simply opened gates for him to go through.

When sorting cattle, we did not rope a cow, pull her through a gate, then release her. We instead opened the gate we wanted her to go through and blocked where we did not want her to go until she eventually found the open gate…the path of least resistance. Likewise, when riding a horse, we don't pull them where we want them to go—we block where we don't want them to go. I'll make an admission here…I get strongly bothered by folks that sit on their butts in the saddle and do nothing but pull on their reins, then claim they can ride. One of my favorite questions to ask folks is, "Are you a rider or a passenger?" A rider's legs, seat, and hands are always engaged in opening and closing pathways for the horse. A passenger sits, pulls, and jerks. (I digress…. Rant over.)

Tom Dorrance shared another quote that kind of goes along these same lines: *If you can get a horse to move away from pressure, why can't you get a horse to move to where there is no pressure?* I thought that was a great revelation—again, *the path of least resistance.* If I'm riding my horse and I'm just letting my legs rest against the sides of the horse with equal pressure so he knows I'm on him, riding him, and supporting him, then if I want him to move left, maybe instead of adding pressure with my right leg, perhaps I could simply release a bit of the steady pressure from my left leg. When there's no pressure there, the "gate" opens. Maybe the horse will go through the open gate. If he does, great! If he doesn't, then I can help him go through it by adding light pressure on the right side.

We should strive for our horses to respond to the softest of pressure. If we really want to refine our communication with them, maybe we need to start off with a "whisper" instead of a "yell." Maybe we need to start with not having pressure applied immediately; maybe we need to simply open a gate so the horse can find his way.

Let's keep in mind that this is about understanding horses. Let's continue to consider that long before humans confined and domesticated horses, they naturally moved from place to place to survive, and they went where things were easiest—where there was good grass, good water, good cover from predators, good shelter from inclement weather, and so on. In other words, horses in the wild moved along the path of least resistance. It was natural for them to do so. Therefore, if we want to maximize our relationship with the horse and develop a sense of trust in him, then perhaps we should help him adapt to the unnatural environments we often place him in by making what we want an easy option along a path of least resistance. Why? Because it's a concept he already understands.

I frequently teach people how to use the path of least resistance while working horses in a round pen when nothing but I can impede their forward movement. As I demonstrate this, I repeat the other phrase I already mentioned in this chapter: *We don't pull a horse where we want him to go, we block where we don't want him to go.* In my years of experience as a professional horseman, helping young horses learn or helping rehabilitate older horses to better understand things we want them to do, I find *the path of least resistance, making the right thing easy and the wrong thing difficult,* and *not pulling a horse where we want him to go, but blocking where we don't want him to go* yield the greatest results. Remember, horses learn from the release of perceived pressure, regardless if that pressure is *implied* or *applied.*

Our goal is to always offer the horse the best deal we can offer him. In equestrian circles, we hear the term *light* a lot. We want our horses to be *light.* What does that mean? It means we want them to respond to the least amount of influence from us as possible. How much lighter can we get than to just create an opening for the horse to go through? Then, if that is not enough, perhaps we should apply a very light amount of pressure to inspire the horse to move. And if *that* doesn't work, we should increase the pressure a bit. And so on and so on. Eventually we will create an uncomfortable situation for the horse in his position, and he will seek a more comfortable one.

I tell folks to *squeeze, bump, kick,* and *kill.* Man, when I say that, I sure see folks' do a double-take! "Did he say kill?" they ask. It's just a shock statement. Of course, I do not mean I want anyone to kill a horse. But I do want the pressure people offer to be believable to the horse. When we ask a horse to perform a task that we are without a doubt confident that he can achieve, we must be persistent, consistent, and progressive in our request. The first time we ask, we simply want the request to be as light and easy as it can be—a *squeeze.* If no response, then we ask a bit more firmly—a *bump.* If no response, we progress to asking more firmly still—a *kick.* Finally, if the horse still does not respond, we must progress to being downright threatening—this is the *kill.*

Now hold on! Don't call the animal rights folks just yet. All I mean is to do whatever it takes to make the horse uncomfortable in the place he is, so that he seeks a response suitable to regain his comfort—it's (here we go…have you been paying attention?) *the path of least resistance.* This is not a new concept to the horse at all. It's a language the horse fully understands. It's natural to him. Let's think about the process of communication between horses. In their world, they, too, communicate in progressive stages. For example, a horse may begin by moving an ear to get another horse to do what he wants. If that works, fine. If it doesn't, the horse might threaten to bite. Again, if that works, fine. If it doesn't, the first horse might actually bite the other horse. If even *that* doesn't work, the first horse might turn and kick the other one with both hind legs. The first horse's behavior escalates, depending on the reaction of the second horse. They *squeeze, bump, kick,* and *kill.*

Those who dwell on the words "natural horsemanship" must know that the true practice of natural horsemanship is in conflict with what you might term "gentle horsemanship." Sometimes natural horsemanship isn't gentle, just like sometimes horses aren't gentle with each other. It can be and is gentle when it's *communication-refined.* Communication-refined is when we simply open the gate and the horse willingly and readily goes through it. Sometimes, to get that refined, we need to follow up with the squeeze, bump, kick, and kill. We need to be able to realize that in order for the horse to find the path of least resistance, sometimes he has to understand resistance. And he has to understand pressure.

When we were working cattle with my mom, how did we get the cows to find the gate? Number one, they knew where the gate was. Number two, if they didn't find their way to the gate, we'd put pressure on the inside of the pen so they'd seek the way to get to the outside of the pen. We let them find the path of least resistance. And their reward was being released back out in the pasture where there was no pressure.

Even today, anytime I think of or teach about the path of least resistance, I very fondly think of my mom working that sorting gate at the cattle pens during my youth.

CHAPTER 8

DARE YOUR HORSE TO BE GOOD

IF I HAVE said it once I've said it thousands of times, *Let your horse go*. Most of the time when I'm encouraging someone to let her horse go, I am referring to the fact that her reins are too tight and the bit is too engaged in the horse's mouth. However, I can appreciate a rider's concerns when I have to repeat, *Let your horse go*. To the novice and the rider that has had a bad experience on horseback—such as a horse that bolted, spooked, or bucked…or even bucked them off—their concerns about letting their horses go are fear-based. Again, I appreciate that.

Another time I might encourage someone to let the horse go is when a person is quick to correct the horse or corrects him too frequently. I compare this kind of riding to a driver of a vehicle that makes passengers car sick from oversteering or steering abruptly. This driver often has difficulty controlling speed too, speeding up or slowing down, but rarely maintaining a consistent pace. (Have you ever noticed the driver in these situations never gets car sick?) I find this particular scenario is common with the inexperienced or the "Type-A" personality. As you may know, Type-A personalities may be more anxious, impatient, and concerned about time management. These can be great traits and are common in high-achievers. But as my grandmother would say, "Everything in moderation."

Part of being a good horseman is being keenly aware of one's horse at all times. Although having a tight hold on the reins might help you feel more secure in the saddle, the question is, how does it affect the horse? Let's consider for a moment the things that make a horse feel secure. I'd wager the list would include freedom, comfort, confidence, and leadership, perhaps. There are more, but let's consider these four for a moment. A rider that has her reins held too tightly may feel more secure, but how are her actions with her own personal security in mind impacting the security of the horse? The reins being too tightly held is surely uncomfortable for the horse. It restricts his freedom and perhaps diminishes his confidence in his leader (the rider). We know from our basic understanding of horses that their first instinct when they are threatened, insecure, or uncomfortable is flight. They want to escape from where they are to find safety in a more comfortable place. Who could blame them? However, when being ridden by a rider that is the source of their anxiety, what are they to do? They try to communicate their need for relief from the bit or bridle by perhaps dancing or jigging, or tossing their heads and extending their noses. This behavior concerns or frustrates the rider, so the rider might apply more pressure to the reins, thinking it will restrict the horse from being able to jig or toss his head. This only makes the discomfort, and cause of the behavior, worse.

I wonder sometimes if folks fully understand what is going on when a horse tosses his head, for example. What's taking place is the horse is seeking relief from the pressure of the bit or bridle, if only for a fraction of a moment. When a rider has the reins tight and the horse tosses his head, the rider's arms are extended by the pull from the horse for a second. During the brief time the rider's arms move from the extended position back to the bent and braced position, the reins are slack. The horse achieved his own release.

I like to demonstrate this situation at horsemanship clinics. I do so by asking a clinic participant to hold one end of a lead rope while I hold the other. I'll gradually ease the slack out of the rope, then ask the participant to keep the rope tight and not allow slack in the rope nor allow me to pull the participant toward me. If I begin to slowly pull more on my end of the rope inevitably, I will feel my partner in the exercise increase the pull on the opposite end of the rope. However, if I instead pull quickly and abruptly without prior notice, the participant is temporarily caught off guard, and her arm is temporarily extended, or the rope may even slide through her hand a bit. In either scenario, from that moment until she regains her grip on the rope or bends her arm, the rope is slack. During that slack moment, there is no tension in the rope.

In the defense of some riders, they simply do not realize they are pulling on the reins. I'd wager that most people's hands, although extremely sensitive, are not as sensitive as a horse's mouth or nose.

When my wife and I travel together, we frequently hold hands. I'm a horseman. I work with my hands on the ranch in one way or another just about every day—handling ropes, saddles, gates, feed buckets, hay, manure forks, post drivers, pipes, tractor implements, and so much more. My hands are strong, calloused, and rough. My wife, also a very hard worker, does a completely different type of work with her hands. She handles the phone, computer, contracts, folders, cameras, and other elements of our business. Her hands are strong, smooth, and soft. Yet we love to hold each other's hands. Occasionally, while we are holding hands, my wife will readjust her hand in mine. Because my hand is strong, rough, and calloused I often don't realize the grip I have on her strong, smooth, and soft hand. I very much enjoy holding her hand, so I must be keenly aware that her hand in comparison to mine is more sensitive. I must be present in my awareness. When I am not, my grip gets tighter and eventually uncomfortable for my wife. That's when she reminds me with an adjustment.

To earn the privilege and satisfaction of holding my wife's hand, I must remain present and accountable. For a rider to earn the privilege and satisfaction of riding a horse, the rider must remain present and accountable. Those who choose not to be accountable for the discomfort they may be causing a horse might address head-tossing by applying another device, such as a tie-down or a martingale. Both of these can be useful tools for their intended purposes but certainly not for this case. The tie-down or martingale may prevent the horse from tossing his head, but the cause of the behavior still remains. *Address the cause; find the cure.*

It seems it's all a vicious cycle: "If I let go, the horse might run off"…"If I don't let go, the horse will be anxious and want to run off." What to do?

First, the remedy is to break the cycle. Who goes first? Isn't this an age ol' question? Who goes first *in this case* is the one that most desires to be the good leader. The leader in both horsemanship and "humanship" is usually the one that makes the best decisions on behalf of the herd, group, or team. A good leader takes the responsibility and is accountable for teaching, coaching, demonstrating, encouraging, and motivating those around her, *then* has the courage and discipline to afford others the *accountability* and *responsibility* to do that which has been taught, coached, or demonstrated.

To be successful at any level—at achieving a small task or a long-term goal—there's no escaping accountability and responsibility. How much accountability and responsibility is another question, as some folks can handle a lot and some not so much. We have to be really honest about the type of person we are and what we can handle. There are those who want to handle or control every aspect of life—everything they do and everything others do that might affect them—to the point that they may be difficult to be around. Then there are those who feel like they need to be in control, not because they are fueling their egos, but because they are protecting themselves from the things they fear.

Very few times did my children's mother and I differ in our way of raising our girls. However, one night my oldest daughter called, very upset and crying. Jazmin explained that her mother and stepfather had fastened her bedroom window shut with screws so that it could not be opened.

"Why"? I asked. Of course, I immediately thought the window being secured as Jaz described was potentially dangerous. Knowing my ex-wife was very cautious and safety-conscious, I could not imagine why she would choose to have Jaz's window shut in such a way.

Jazmin went on to explain that a week or so prior, her close friend sneaked out of her house through her bedroom window to spend time with friends after curfew. My ex-wife and Jazmin's friend's mom were also friends and attended the same church, so of course the "sneaking-out incident" was discussed between them. When asked what action was taken, the friend's mother said they had screwed their daughter's window shut. To them, the problem was solved. So my ex-wife and her husband decided to be proactive. Rather than using the situation as an opportunity to discuss the situation with Jazmin, they chose what they believed was a preventive measure.

As I've mentioned before, our girls were incredibly easy to raise. Both were very good students, responsible, and never got in trouble. With these facts in mind, I questioned as to what justified fastening Jaz's window shut with screws. After all, it was Jazmin's *friend* that sneaked out, *not* Jazmin. Why, then, such a reaction?

Let me emphasize that my ex-wife was and is a great mother to our girls.

Her reaction in this situation was based on fear. She was fearful that the girls were approaching their teenage years. She was fearful that they might do things other teenaged girls do. She was fearful that Jaz might be more influenced by the behavior of her friends than the foundation of her upbringing. Lastly, she was fearful that Jaz couldn't be trusted. However, the reaction and decision to fasten the window shut demonstrated a lack of trust in a few areas. Jazmin certainly felt that her mother didn't trust her. Because she had always been such a good and trustworthy child, this was extremely difficult for Jaz to understand. As result, Jaz lost trust in her mother. And what about my ex's trust in herself? Could she have truly trusted and believed in the foundation she'd laid for the girls if she couldn't *let go* and trust that her years of "training" would work? In order to know if one's "training" is effective, it must be tested. The thing about testing is that it yields feedback. Sometimes the feedback may not be what we want, but it nevertheless usually informs us about our strengths and weaknesses. My ex demonstrated a lack of trust in herself and her own preparedness for such a situation, and therefore her fear of what the feedback of the test of her "training" might look like caused her to make a choice that caused her daughter to lose trust in her.

We must be willing to test, let go, dare to be good, and by all means have trust—in ourselves and in others.

Some of the most successful people I've met are the Henry Fords of the world. For a particular project in college, I studied Henry Ford, who is credited with the concept of the mass production of automobiles. Now, Henry Ford was not known as a "book smart" guy. He was very brilliant in understanding mechanics, engineering, and processes, even though his only formal education was in bookkeeping. However, when Ford was releasing a new product or making corporate changes or whatever the case may be, he would hold press conferences. Snide reporters would occasionally poke fun at Mr. Ford by asking questions to which they figured he probably wouldn't know the answers. One day he put a stop to that practice when he said to one such rude reporter, "Young man, I don't know the answer to that question, but I have over one hundred people that work for me that do. Next question."

In my humble opinion, this was a brilliant response from Mr. Ford. It said that he was done with responding to petty, irrelevant questions. Most importantly it said that he understood the purpose of *roles*. It was not his role to know everything. He trusted others in his company to know things. Mr. Ford was smart enough to know his job and allow other people to do their jobs. Together they formed a stronger team. Of course, as the leader of the company he is ultimately accountable and responsible for every employee's actions, failures, and successes. Leaders must have great commitment while also having great trust in those around them.

The same can be applied to horsemanship. In order for me to be a good horseman, I must know I can't do the horse's job. I've only got two legs. There's no way for me to move around nearly as well, with as much strength and athleticism, as a horse can. I could never pull a plow as well or as efficiently as a horse. I could not carry a passenger as easily as a horse. I could not cut a cow from a herd as effectively as a horse. I could not go over the jumps that horses do. I could not run the races that horses run. These things and countless others are strengths of the horse. God blessed horses with size, speed, strength, stamina, and the intelligence to be trained. So, what strengths do *we* have? Among many more, one of our best strengths is the ability to think and use logic, which we do much better than the horse. I frequently say that God blessed horses with a brain the size of our fist, but God blessed humans with a brain the size of *both* our fists. What that tells me is maybe we can use our strengths to teach the horse to use his strengths—and together we can achieve remarkable things as a team. To do so takes trust, courage, discipline, self-confidence, and faith.

It seems that my job for a couple of decades has been to help people discover or advance their leadership and communication skills by helping them use skills they already have or develop those they do not. When leadership, communication, trust, courage, self-discipline, and faith are present, and they hear me say to them, *Let your horse go*, they should have the confidence to let their horse go and *dare the horse to be good*. The sometimes not-so-simple act of letting go and giving those around us the opportunity to do something well is a step in developing trust in one's self, others, and one's program or process. Learn to develop that trust by strengthening your personal skills to the point where you have confidence in others. Where they are weak, help them be strong. Where you are weak, work to improve.

Back in my competitive days, I developed a strong winning reputation by going to some challenging events—for example, ranch horse versatility, which consists of four classes: ranch trail, ranch riding, working ranch horse, and ranch cutting. There are several components within each of the four individual classes, and a competitor is scored on each component or maneuver. The winner of the overall versatility competition is the individual with the highest cumulative average. Anyway, I was going to a lot of those competitions around the country and consistently finishing in the top three at each event. People asked how I did it. The remarkable thing was, at times, the horses my competition was riding had two, sometimes three more years of training than the horses I was competing on.

So how did I do it?

I was very fortunate as a freshman to be part of the Austin College football team that won a national championship, and then two years later, to be on the Lone Star Conference championship football team at East Texas State University (now Texas A&M-Commerce). Being part of multiple championship teams, I began to realize that success wasn't about having the most talent, but that we played the best as a unit consistently over time. Strengths and weaknesses were constantly being evaluated. Practices were focused on being honest about those strengths and weaknesses and how they pertained to each player, each position, each play. The most successful were those who made the necessary changes and increased their strengths.

How does this relate to horse show competitions? Well, the team was me and the horse. I couldn't do the horse's role, and he couldn't do my role, which meant we had to learn to trust each other. This also meant we had to be keenly aware of and honest about each other's strengths and weaknesses. As the leader, I had to determine what my horse's strengths were, prepare him well, and dare him to be good. I also had to be keenly aware of and honest about where the horse's weaknesses were, and during the course of a competition, protect those weaknesses, rather than expose them.

The other side of the coin was, as part of the team, I had to be honest with myself about my strengths and weaknesses in regard to the competition. On "game day," so to speak, what could I do to accentuate our strengths to get the best possible scores? Meanwhile what could be done to survive our weaknesses, protect the scores, and not get penalties?

Our success was based on knowing our strengths and weaknesses, and daring my horse to be good.

Of course, I don't mean "daring" like "taunting." I mean giving the horse the opportunity to do well with preparation and then allowing him to be good in the moment. The results are unbelievably rewarding. The results may also be very telling. They tell us what we need to go back and work on.

I don't think I would have put the pieces of the puzzle together and found success in competitive horse sports had it not been for my college football days. They taught me:

- Know what you want and work hard to develop the skills necessary to succeed at what you want.

- Know your strengths and weaknesses and surround yourself with others that have talents and skills toward achieving the things you want.

- Communicate your ultimate goals.

- Set up yourself and those around you to be successful by preparing the best you can.

- Have faith in your program then let go so each part of the team can perform the respective roles.

- Dare your teammates to be good. Dare your horse to be good.

CHAPTER 9

FIRM HANDS MAKE A LIGHT HORSE

THE END OF the 1980s brought about many and major life changes for me. In just a few action-packed years, I had finished college, gone to work as a sales rep in the tech industry, ended a bad relationship, started rodeoing again, started training horses again, started a new relationship, and oh yeah… moved to New Zealand. Yep, I sold everything I could sell—my new truck, horse trailer, horses, saddles, boat and fishing gear—then packed a few pieces of luggage, boarded a plane with my new girlfriend, and flew to the "Land of the Long White Cloud" and home of the kiwi. This was an incredibly adventurous life experience for me. Prior to the trip, I had been out of the country only twice before, both on spring break visits to Mexico, our good neighbor to the south. The first time, I literally walked from Texas to the small Mexican border town of Matamoras. The second was a short flight to a quaint but growing resort area of Mexico. Apart from that, I had been out of Texas no more times than I could count on one hand. Therefore, the decision to move to New Zealand, for me, was colossal.

My girlfriend's family lived in Auckland, the largest city in New Zealand. The city, too, was a major adjustment for me because I was a true red-white-and-blue, Lone Star country boy from rural Texas. To me, big cities were places one only went to for quick day trips, or to shop for things not typically found in rural stores, or to get better medical attention than could be had in small town clinics or hospitals. Everything was new to me—the people, the accents, the vehicles (steering wheels were on the right side), the roadways (vehicles drove on the left), the being surrounded by water. My first few days in New Zealand were overwhelming and amazing.

However, all too soon the reality of finding employment set in. I was a foreigner. I had to get a work permit. I knew no one and had no inside connections or leads on jobs. I did have an education and a good employment history with proof of results. Eventually I was hired to be a purchasing officer for a regional airline. Accepting the job meant yet another move, this time within country, but another move, nonetheless. Auckland is located on a very thin peninsula-like area in the northern part of New Zealand's North Island. We would be moving to Nelson, in the northern part of the South Island of New Zealand.

Being hired by Air Nelson (later to be renamed as Air New Zealand Link) and moving to Nelson was an absolute blessing. The income from the job was good and the location was like New Zealand's version of East Texas. At the time, the actual city of Nelson was no larger than a few of the small towns I was accustomed to back home. The region was known for agriculture and fishing. There were numerous fruit and vegetable farms, small cattle operations, and dairy farms. In other words, it was all very similar to what I'd grown up with.

After we'd been in the region a few weeks and I'd settled into my job at the airport, we began to reach out and socialize with the locals a bit. In our attempt to both meet new people and hold on to a bit of the familiar, we opted to attend a "country-and-western club" one evening. First, we were shocked to discover that it in no way resembled what might be referred to as a "country-and-western club" in Texas. In Texas, we'd picture a dimly lit smoke-filled room with a stage, dance floor, and of course a bar. When we walked in the door in Nelson's "country-and-western club," it was more like…well, a club. Folks were sitting around fold-out, rectangular tables in a brightly lit room. There was a band set up, but no bar—just a table with homemade refreshments and numerous types of juices, hot tea, and coffee. It was like we were newcomers to a country church. People noticed us right away and began introducing themselves and taking us around from one table to another. (I'm certain the kiwis are some of the most friendly and polite people I've ever known.) Everyone loved my Texas drawl, although I never realized I had one until I moved to where no one else sounds like me.

After an incredibly entertaining evening full of kiwi renditions of classic country music presented in an open-mic-type format, it was time for my girl-friend and I to retire. As we wrapped up our goodbyes, I thought it wise for me to visit the men's room before the short drive back to our neighborhood and bungalow-style house. While in the restroom, I could have sworn I heard another guy saying something to someone else about team roping. (Mind you, I still wasn't completely accustomed to the dialect of New Zealanders.) So, when I finished my personal business, I turned to see a long tall fella standing at the wash basin, talking with another guy who looked like he could be his brother. When I say "long tall," I mean this young man was six foot five and weighed slightly more than a broom handle.

I spoke right up and asked, "Did I hear you say something about team roping?"

Man! Did his face light up when I said those words with my Texas drawl. He responded immediately and enthusiastically with, "Ah yeah, mate. My mates and me will be meetin' at Laury McVicar's place there in Hope to do a wee bit of ropin'. Do you do a little ropin' yourself there, mate?"

"Yes, sir. I definitely do a little roping." As I washed and dried my hands, it was apparent that the long tall fella and the guy who looked like his brother thoroughly enjoyed my drawl. We introduced ourselves (they were Wayne and Marty), shook hands, exchanged phone numbers, and they shared the address to Laury McVicar's arena in a small community named Hope, where I was to meet them the next day.

Mr. Laury McVicar was old enough to be at least my father but perhaps more like a grandfather. In fact, I still jokingly but fondly tell folks that Laury was like my surrogate grandfather in New Zealand. He was wise, experienced, direct, and confident enough to tell you his opinion without imposing himself on you too much. I was still quite young in my horsemanship journey then. In fact, I'm embarrassed by how little I actually knew about horses at that point in my life. Granted, I was no slouch, by any stretch, but oh my goodness—I was only scratching the surface. I now know what one of my mentors meant when at the ripe ol' age of eighty-six he confessed, "I'm afraid I'm gonna die before I learn all I want to learn about these darned horses."

Laury and I clicked right away and ended up spending countless hours talking about horses, horsemanship, roping, and the price of tea in China. Laury was forever curious. Because I was an American, a Texan, and the new guy in town, he wanted to pick my brain on my philosophy of horse training, riding, and the bloodlines I liked. It seems we conversed about every topic you can think about that had to do with horses.

Laury loved to watch me ride and was always asking questions about what I did, when I did it, why I did it, and what the timing of it was. He frequently complimented me on my hands. Horse trainers, in particular, looked at other trainers' hands, their balance, and their legs. Something my real grandfather shared with me a long time ago was to "always know enough to stay out of the horse's way." Good horsemen watch to see what riders will do to set their horses up to be successful. If they do set them up properly, will they get out of the way and let their horses do what they ask? Laury was most definitely one of those inquisitive guys, watching everything I did, and he kept noticing and commenting that I had really soft hands, soft legs, and good balance. This meant my legs were always in good timing with the horse as far as getting responses and then taking my cues away at just the right time. He also noticed that even though in general my hands were very soft, I would apply pressure very firmly when necessary, but was quick to release that pressure when the horse either did what I wanted or made an attempt to do what I wanted.

One day while taking a break and having some tea (I learned to like hot tea while living in New Zealand), Laury looked at me and said, "You know, Van, 'firm hands make a light horse,' and the horses you ride are light."

At first I thought, *What does that mean?* People had always said I had "soft hands" and "light hands." Now this guy, who I keenly respected, was using the term "firm hands."

Once he planted that seed in my mind, I began to think more about it, and I noticed that every time I was working with a horse, I would be as firm as necessary. I think that's one of the biggest things that people miss out on when they are training horses. They want the horse to be light, therefore *they* are really light. The problem is, sometimes you have to be firm enough to cause the horse to make a change. The key is to start light and increase firmness slowly and gradually until the response you were seeking is achieved or at least tried. Then you can back off and be light again. Without being aware of it, that's what I was doing. I was doing what I needed to do to get the result that I wanted. Until Laury had mentioned it in the way he had, I hadn't given it much thought. After that, though, it became a useful tool for me. *Being firm to be light* became an everyday practice for me. When riding a horse, I would think, *How firm do I have to be and how light can I be?* That became my goal. I want to be committed to being as firm as I had to be to get the result I wanted, but then the next time, ease off a little and see if I could still get the same result. So, on a scale from one to ten, if I got the result being a firm ten, next time, could I get the same result with a nine? I may only get to a nine that lesson, but the horse was learning. He was ten percent better. If I keep doing that exact process, eventually I can get the horse to respond to just a suggestion. Which reminds me of yet another quote I learned from Mr. Tom Dorrance: "Be as light as possible but as firm as necessary."

It wasn't until Laury planted the seed that I became aware of being firm to achieve lightness. From that time on it not only put me on a path to improving my own horsemanship with each ride, but it put me in a position where I could help others with their horsemanship. It was something I could use, not only as a quote and reminder, but in the form of practices that would help students better understand and perhaps put them on a trail toward better horsemanship.

"Firm hands make a light horse" applies to daily life, too. The first thing I think of is being a father. As I've already mentioned, I'm often asked how my daughters turned out so good, and number one, they have a great mom, and number two, and as I've said before, I think my years of horsemanship helped me be a better dad. Up until I became a father, the only experience I ever had with disciplining others was with horse training. I began to use the exact same practices with my daughters. It wasn't always on a conscious level, but sometimes it was.

It's what I call in child-rearing *ask, suggest, and tell*. First, I'm going to ask in a kind way for something to be done and hopefully get an affirmative response. If not, I'm going to suggest something be done. Still nothing? Then, by golly, I'm going to *tell* you to do it. The key is to get a little more firm as one goes and watch for a little change (hopefully, a positive one). And once the child responds to the *tell*, well, you can back off to the *ask* again.

I've also used "firm to be light" in other relationships, such as in business dealings. Know what you want and ask for it in the easiest, nicest way possible. Hopefully, you'll get what you want. If not, be committed to stepping up the ask along the way.

When I think of *firm hands make a light horse*, I also consider how being *firm but fair* is very important. The term "respect" comes to mind. I think you get a better response from those around you when you are firm, and people tend to respect you if you are very consistent and very fair.

When I was growing up, everything about my stepfather was abrupt. He'd walk in the door, and one minute, he'd be quiet and calm, and the next minute he'd erupt for no apparent reason. We could never trust his mood. We always acted and reacted in fear. We did things in fear of what his reaction would be if we didn't do them. We would do things in fear that if they weren't done to his satisfaction, his reaction might be violent.

If you start out abrupt and stay abrupt in your relationship with a horse, he is always going to expect abrupt behavior from you, and what you are going to get back from him will be abrupt (anxious) behavior. If instead you are consistent in how you ask with a progression from light to firm, horses (and people) will trust the fact that by the time you get to the point of being firm, then you have been fair in the process. You've earned their respect and earned their trust and earned the idea that you're being as fair as possible. The practice of being firm but fair reminds me of keeping promises: Perhaps when asking a horse to go from a standstill to a walk, a rider could think, *I promise not to put pressure on you to make you go, but I also promise that if you don't go, I'll put pressure on you.*

As a dad and a professional horseman, I frequently had to adjust my riding and training time with my responsibilities associated with having small children. One day while returning client phone calls, I was somewhat distracted while watching Jazmin and Britni. As young energetic children close to the same age will do, they were romping and playing, although for the most part being respectfully quiet during my calls. At one point, however, their rambunctiousness turned into what seemed like a version of "hallway chicken." The girls would get on opposite ends of the hallway and run toward each other, then at the last moment, dodge to miss one another. Seeing what this was going to lead to, I placed my hand over the phone and whispered loudly (parents know what this is), "Stop that! Y'all are going to run into each other and hurt yourselves." I then returned to the call as if I'd not missed a lick of the conversation.

A few minutes later the temptation of the fun they had been having overwhelmed the girls, and they went at it again. Once more, I placed my hand over the phone and whispered a little more loudly this time, and I'm reasonably sure I gave a parent-faced threatening look: "Girls! Stop passing each other in the hallway! Y'all are going to hurt yourselves!" And…back to my call.

Eventually…*BAM!*

If you've raised kids, you know exactly what it sounds like when they either bump each other's heads or bump their heads on something. That's what I heard, followed by deafening silence, immediately followed by blood-curdling screams.

"I'll call you right back," I said to my client as I hung up the phone and dashed toward the hallway all in one smooth athletic move my former college football coaches would have been proud of. In two steps I was confronted by one small red-headed child and one smaller blonde-headed child walking toward me with similar features…red faces, streams of tears down the cheeks (and more welling up in their big sad eyes), and of course, the feature that was new and most distinctive smack dab in the middle of their foreheads: matching egg-shaped knots that seemed to be growing and changing colors with each passing moment.

Well, the consequences of their actions and their failure to heed my warnings had already been paid. After consoling them for a moment and checking for concussions, because that's what parents are supposed to do, I asked the girls what they thought I should do about them ignoring my orders not to run in the hallway. By this time, I was sitting on the couch with two tiny people standing before me, trying their best to suck it up and get control of their snuffling. I bit a hole in my lip trying not to laugh because they were so darned cute! But I had parental duty…I asked again, "Hmm, what do y'all think I should do?"

Doing her dead-level best to be a good big sister, Jaz looked up at me, fighting back more tears, and said in about as big a way as she could muster, "Well, I guess we need a whoopin."

Oh, my goodness…I felt my body shudder as I fought as hard as I ever had to hold back the laughter. You see, my girls had never had a spanking in their lives. So, for Jaz to say this was not only shocking, it was hilariously funny. Not just that she said it but the way Britni's head snapped around to look at her sister as if to say, "Girl! Are you crazy?"

Somehow, I was able to force these words from my mouth without a chuckle, "Well, Jazmin Bree, that's not exactly what I had in mind, but if you think that's what I should do, then I guess that's what we'll do." I asked her sister, "Britni Skye, do you think y'all need a spanking?"

Britni paused for a long while and finally affirmed with a nod that shook from her blue eyes a few more tears down the tracks of her dimpled cheeks.

"Well, girls, I reckon y'all have come up with a good solution—so, who's going first?"

The tears came back with a vengeance, but Jaz made her daddy proud as she snuffled real hard, held her head up as proud as she could, and boldly proclaimed, "I'm the oldest, so I guess I'll go first." This, to me, spoke volumes about the character, strength, and bravery of my grown up three-year-old little girl.

Each girl got a spanking that day. First Jazmin, then Britni. Mind you, I was about to cry myself because of the bravery and character each of my daughters demonstrated. We'd all been on a rollercoaster of emotions in a short period of time. Fun and laughter, fear and anguish, respect and pride.

Now, just so everyone knows, the spat the girls got that day was just a formality, one could say—no harder than one would slap a mosquito on your own sunburned butt. But, because of the foundation laid out from the beginning of the girls' wee little lives, that firm hand was all it took. That was the first and the last spanking they ever got. The foundation of their upbringing was and is the foundation that has helped me achieve more than I ever thought possible in my career as a professional horseman. Thank you, Laury McVicar for sharing with me, *Firm hands make a light horse.* They make darned good daughters, too.

CHAPTER 10

BEND 'EM TO KEEP 'EM STRAIGHT

WHILE ALLOWING A young horse to stand and rest between exercises, I felt my cell phone vibrate. *Perfect timing*, I thought. I dug the phone from my front left pocket and responded as I usually do early in the day, "Good morning, this is Van."

On the other end of the call a friendly female voice explained that she was with the Stock Horse of Texas (SHOT) and they were having a show and clinic in Abilene and wanted to know if I would be one of the clinicians at the event. I was honored by the inquiry, and after verifying that my calendar was open on that particular weekend, I proudly agreed to do the event. As we were about to end the call, the young lady asked if I would mind having another clinician work with me. I quickly let her know I had no problem with sharing the arena with another clinician but I did ask, "Who will I be working with?" When she said my co-clinician would be Mr. Jack Brainard, I'm sure I grew taller in the saddle. I ended the call, slipped the phone back into my pocket, squeezed the colt off into a canter, and joyously continued his morning training session.

Mr. Jack, as most folks refer to him, had been a hero of mine from the time I was about eight years old. I first met him at a 4-H horse judging event in Denton, Texas. In those days, my mother and stepfather were 4-H leaders for a small group of young horse enthusiasts in Hunt County. To be in 4-H, one is supposed to be nine years old. I was only eight. I tagged along to every class and learned the horse judging information, just as the older kids did. In fact,

I'm pretty certain I studied harder and paid closer attention than most of them did. The young teenagers were distracted by being smart with each other and joking around. They were all great kids, just typical for their age group. I, on the other hand, had no idea what they were laughing and kidding about most of the time, therefore wasn't as distracted.

The goal behind all the work of learning to judge horses was to attend the state of Texas 4-H Horse Judging Competition. Our region was one of the largest and toughest regions in Texas. Our regional competition was to be held at the home of then world champion cutting horse Cutter Bill, owned by Mr. Rex Cauble.

On the day of the big judging event in Denton, we were all excited. Upon arrival, our team was instructed as to how and where to register. My mother and stepfather walked around with each of our team members and made sure all were signed up at the appropriate tables and able to compete both as a team and individuals. (Of course, I tagged along and did just as all the big kids did.) As the judging competition started, groups were formed, and kids went all over the facility to judge different classes and then turn in their score cards. I again tagged along and did as the big kids did.

At the end of the day, all the score cards were tallied, and it was time to proclaim the winners and announce who would be advancing on to the final competition. Minutes into the ceremony, the announcer said as plain as day that Van Hargis of the Hunt County 4-H Club would be advancing to the Finals. Of course, I was excited as the crowd clapped in congratulations but…all the kids in our club, along with my mother and stepfather, simply froze and stared at me in disbelief. Mom bent down to whisper something in my ear just as the announcer asked me to step forward to get my judging cards for the Finals. I shook my head, indicating I couldn't step forward. The crowd went quiet and the announcer looked puzzled. I had to confess, "I'm too young; I'm only eight."

It was apparent by the expressions on my parents faces that they were torn between being proud that I had performed so well and embarrassed that I had registered for the competition with the rest of the group. I couldn't accept the award nor could I advance to the finals. It wasn't right. Rules were rules, and they clearly stated that 4-H participants were to be nine years old or older.

I was disappointed to the point of almost crying as I stood there silent with my head down, holding back tears, when I heard a voice say, "Fine job, young man. Any young man that can judge horses as good as you deserves to make it to the Finals." The speaker took my hand and offered, "You can go with me and judge the horses in the Finals." I had no idea who the man was; I simply knew he was quiet, kind, and gracious enough to take me around and let me judge the last classes of the day at the regional 4-H horse judging competition. Of course, my score cards would not be tallied this time, but I truly appreciated the opportunity.

It was much later that I learned the man was Mr. Jack Brainard. He's been a hero to me ever since.

As I grew older, I began to realize Mr. Jack was a true master of horsemanship. He was not only a master of training horses, but also training people. Jokingly, a lot of us trainers say that Jack Brainard has probably trained more trainers than most of us have trained horses. I've always had tremendous respect for him, and it was a great blessing that he and I had the opportunity to work together at the Stock Horse of Texas clinic in Abilene.

The clinic was quite full with participants; therefore, to be as efficient and proficient as possible, it was decided that we'd divide the arena in half. I'd instruct riders on my half of the arena, and Mr. Jack would do likewise for those on his half of the arena. Because Mr. Jack and I were on horseback, we would meander around the clinic participants to better communicate and demonstrate. Occasionally we'd find ourselves standing side by side, facing our respective ends of the arena.

It was on one of those occasions that a participant on my end of the arena was having difficulty with her horse. Her mare was being very rude and pushy on the bridle. I shouted out some things to the rider about softening her horse by bending her horse around to get the mare to be more responsive to the bit. "Firm hands make a light horse!" I called. I went on to explain how and why to do what I was instructing, as well as the result she should be working to achieve.

Out of the corner of my eye, I saw Mr. Jack shaking his head as I instructed the student. I thought I must have said something wrong. At first I was embarrassed, figuring I'd said something wrong in front of one of my heroes. I leaned and reached back to my belt, turning my microphone off, and I asked Jack if he'd turn his off, too. He did, and so I asked him if I had said something wrong.

"No," he said. "Why?"

I told him I'd seen him shaking his head when I was shouting instructions at the lady with the mare.

"Van," he replied. "I'm just afraid I'm going to die before I learn everything I want to learn about these darned horses."

At the time, Mr. Jack was approximately eighty-five years old, and as I previously said, he'd trained more trainers than most of us had trained horses. How humbling it was to know that a man as accomplished as Mr. Jack and a horseman of his age was still seeking to learn.

Later that night, Mr. Jack and I were having supper together, and I asked him what he meant about "what more he had to learn about horses."

"Well," he said. "I like what you said to that lady, and I learned something from it. I was thinking, 'Why do we tell people to bend and flex their horses?'"

I said I wasn't sure, and I started spouting out all the things trainers tell people: "We want to bend them to keep them softer in the face," "We want to bend them to teach them to respect the bridle," "We want to bend them to supple them." All these were very common and typical sayings in horse training. Jack agreed, but he had a look on his face indicating I still hadn't answered his question.

"All those things are right," he said. "But there's more."

In an effort to satisfy him and appease and impress my hero, I rattled off several more reasons as to why we would bend and flex a horse. Again he said all my responses were correct.

28 & 29. Jazmin Bree Hargis at around seventeen months old (above), and Britni Skye Hargis at about twelve months old (below). ⅋

30 & 31. Jazmin (above) and Britni (below) all grown up on their wedding days. I did dual duty for each. Not only did I give them away, I also presided as minister and officiated the marriage ceremonies. ⚑

32. At the Denver Market hosted by the Western & English Sales Association, presenting my first designed saddle built by Billy Cook, pictured with me. His wife was the first paying customer of my horse training career. Ꮗ

33. In the mid 1990s, I found success in what was, at the time, a relatively new competition called Versatility Ranch Horse, and began to give clinics at my ranch in Sulphur Springs, Texas. As you can see, they were very popular as the sport caught on. Ꮗ

34. I made a name for myself in Versatility Ranch Horse. Here I'm showing a client's horse in Glenrose, Texas, in the early 2000s.

35 & 36. I'm on a Friesian stallion in Kansas in 1999 or 2000.

37. With two of the greatest horsemen of our time…Craig Johnson (left) and Martin Black (right). These two are more than colleagues; they are mentors.

38. I have traveled North America teaching horsemanship clinics. At this one at Equine Affaire in West Springfield, Massachusetts, in 2016, I worked with a young horse in the round pen and demonstrated how to put a first ride on without stress.

39. The best part of my career is running into heroes along the way. Mr. Larry Mahan is a multi-time World Champion All-Around Cowboy. He is also a student of horsemanship and a phenomenal horseman.

40. With Mr. Mike Cardwell of East Texas at a clinic not far from his home. Only a few months before he passed after a long battle with cancer, Mike reminded me that I had started colts for him for twenty-five years. Where does the time go?

41. With my sweet grandmother Della Hay a few weeks before her passing. 🤘

42. In 2015, I was blessed to have this remarkable woman, Melanie Marie, marry me. It says a lot for her patience and tolerance as I had been a bachelor for quite a long time! 🤘

43. Riding a three-year-old stallion at a facility I had leased just outside of Victoria, Texas, in 2015, after moving there from Sulphur Springs. ᵛꟼ

44. With "Skeeter," helping folks at a clinic. ᵛꟼ

45. On "Scooter," halter-breaking a few babies. I emphasize roping and handling babies with a breakaway hondo. It makes you learn to be light and soft while applying enough pressure to get a response from them.

46. Working to get the right shot during a video session.

47. Softening a tough colt at a clinic in southern Arizona. 🐂

48. "Cadi," a 2017 gelding by a stallion I started a few years earlier, earned his right to stay in my program. Rather than send him home to the client… I bought him. 🐂

49. With my mother, Carolyn Sue Stockton, in 2018.

50. Mr. Jack Brainard, the "Master of Lead Changes." Mr. Jack was a major influence in my professional career. He did his last clinic at the age of ninety-nine and died at one hundred.

51. Meeting and listening to Mr. Tom Dorrance at a clinic in Texas hosted by my mentor Jack Brainard forever changed my horsemanship practice. Later Mr. Jack arranged for me to spend ten days with Mr. Tom to work with and study horses. Those were ten incredibly enlightening days, for which I'll forever be grateful.
Photo courtesy of Emily Kitching, Eclectic Horseman Magazine.

52. Ray Hunt undoubtedly was a major influence on the advancement of horsemanship in general and certainly a major influence in my horsemanship understanding and application.
Photo courtesy of Emily Kitching, Eclectic Horseman Magazine.

53, 54, & 55. Training horses is still something I love to do every day. I am blessed to have our ranch in Texas and a means to using my spiritual gift.

56. When I know I've helped someone by helping that person learn to work with horses, there's nothing more I need.

"But what you are really saying is that we bend our horses to keep them straight."

I thought, *Wow! That is true.*

So the nuts and bolts of it was, the real answer was, when you peel back all the layers, "We bend them to keep them straight." And why straight? When a horse is straight, he is physically more capable to do what we want him to do. He is stronger and more balanced when he is straight, and every maneuver we want him to do, he can do better if he is balanced, stronger, and straight. If we bend him, the horse's reward is when we let him go. When we release him and let him go, he seeks to be straight. It's where he wants to be. He will seek out straightness.

Now, please let me clarify something that often gets confused when straightness is discussed in horse performance. Firstly, what it does *not* mean is straight like a straight line. *Straightness* in performance horsemanship refers to *full correct balance*. For example, how can a horse's body be literally straight when traveling a small circle? The fact is, a horse cannot be literally straight when traveling a circle. What, then, is meant by straightness when traveling a small circle? A good way to describe this is to imagine a perfect circle drawn on the arena floor. Now imagine a horse walking on that circle. Now imagine three very specific points perfectly aligned on that circle. Those points are the horse's poll, withers, and tail head. In other words, the arc of the horse perfectly aligns with the arc of the circle. When a horse can do this and maintain its rhythm and balance, then it is collected and straight. The horse would be "straight" on the circle. Straightness is synonymous with balanced and collected.

When Mr. Jack told me that we bend a horse to keep him straight, he was referring to so much more than the obvious. When we bend a horse, we are teaching the horse to be softer, more supple, and more responsive, and therefore, perhaps, more controllable in various areas of the body. When we can control more body parts, we greatly increase the odds of controlling the *whole body*—the whole horse.

On the other hand, we can purposefully move parts of the horse's body out of position to perhaps exercise and condition that specific body part; therefore, when we stop exercising and conditioning, the horse will seek out the more comfortable and natural position, which will be the balanced position. (The position that is on the path of least resistance.)

Mr Jack's explanation of straightness taught me that sometimes the obvious isn't clear enough. We have to know the true purpose of something to really understand it. Once we truly understand the purpose, it gives us a better idea of the direction we should go in order to achieve our goals. The general answers as to why we bend and flex our horses were all good and correct, but it was better if we peeled the layers back and got down to the real meaning. Doing so gave our whole journey a clearer purpose.

I began to think about every exercise I ask a horse to do. What was the long-term benefit? What was the true purpose for doing the exercise? Did I have a real understanding of where this exercise was leading? Perhaps another and very important concept to consider was: *Did the horse and I want the same thing?* For instance, consider for a moment that we all want our horses to be comfortable, balanced, and collected. Funny thing is…the horse wants the same thing. So, if what we want is the same, why do we struggle to obtain or achieve it? Perhaps it's because of the unnatural state of a human riding the horse, which alters the horse's ability to travel straight, balanced, and collected.

If a lesson is not leading to something productive, why am I doing it? It's probably going to aggravate the horse and frustrate me, too. If I understand the ultimate purpose, on the other hand, it will give me an idea of why we do the exercises we do. In the case of bending a horse to keep him straight, ultimately, it was about motivating and conditioning the horse to seek out the easier job and be efficient.

Throughout my horsemanship career, I've claimed that I train at one hundred and twenty percent so that one hundred percent seems easy. I learned this from college football. We never ran in a game as much as we ran in practice. Our coaches trained us to be aware of efficiency and to seek it out while simultaneously over-conditioning us so that we had the strength and the stamina to do our jobs with ease. For example, I might work on softness and responsiveness while cantering a circle by asking the horse to keep his body on the circle while flexing his head and neck to the inside of the circle or to the outside of the circle (one hundred and twenty percent). Therefore, when I release the horse, he will seek out a more efficient position, which will be straight on the circle (one hundred percent). A similar example might be walking a line down the rail in an arena, then asking the horse to move his hips or haunches in off the rail, as if asking the horse to two-track. This might be a great exercise to achieve numerous things—such as responsiveness to leg aids, maintaining cadence in stride, and more—but at its simplest, two-tracking is more difficult than walking straight, balanced, and collected (one hundred and twenty percent). Therefore, when the horse two-tracks correctly, I'll release him and allow him to walk straight (one hundred percent). In fact, the horse will seek out straightness. So, *we bend 'em to keep 'em straight.*

Perhaps the same is true in our everyday lives. I recall a client coming out to the ranch for her regular riding lesson on one of my performance horses. As she approached the arena, she began telling me that she'd had an extremely difficult week, and she simply wanted an easy, less challenging, and less stressful lesson. Now this client was as good as gold and rode well, but I had to frequently remind her to let go and trust her posture and trust her horse. She was often too dependent on the bit and reins. So, I was inspired with an idea: After she mounted my mare and was situated in the saddle, I eased my horse up alongside and dropped the headstall off the mare she was on, explaining that since she wanted to have a less stressful ride, I'd give her one less thing to manage and be concerned about.

Without the bridle and reins to be concerned with, my client instead was forced to be more aware of her seat, posture, balance, rhythm, and leg position while she walked, trotted, and cantered circles in the arena. Note that she wasn't allowed to ride random circles. I had her ride circles where and when I prescribed. It was her best ride on my place. In other words, her goal was to be a better rider, and my goal was for her to learn to let go and trust herself and trust her horse. That day I "bent" her to "straighten" her. I had her ride without a bit and reins to demonstrate to her that she didn't need them. When she relied more on clearly communicating with other resources, such as her entire body and mind, she was less dependent on only one form of communication. (Please know that in my professional opinion, my client was very much prepared for that day, as was my mare. I would not use such an approach unless it was safe for both rider and horse.)

In my profession, at least eighty-five percent of my clients are professional women in their late thirties to sixties, and occasionally, even a few more mature. Often they are experiencing issues with their horses because they simply don't know what to do next or they are dealing with other things that are going on in their lives. Many times, the personal issues they are struggling with are revealed in their experiences with their horses. My job, then, is to "bend them"—to help them discover that the cause for one might be the same as for the other. Resolve one and the other might be relieved as well. How? Start peeling layers. Get to the the root of the issues they are experiencing with their horses.

A good number of years ago a lady from Quitman, Texas, called and asked if I would help find a horse for her. She explained that her job was challenging and that she was experiencing difficult times at home with her teenaged son. She went on to say that what made her feel free and relaxed as a young girl was her experiences with her grandfather's horse. Therefore, she decided that perhaps having a horse of her own might help her cope with the stresses of her job and in her household.

In an effort to determine her horsemanship experience and skill level, I invited the woman to my facility to work with a horse or two. At first, I simply had her catch one of my horses. It was quickly revealed that her knowledge and experience with horses was very little. She made several mistakes from the very beginning. Her approach to the horse was very abrupt at first, then shifted to a sneaky slow movement with her hand extended, as if she were offering a treat. She spoke in a tone as if she was sugar-coating a bad event: "Come here…come on, baby. I'm not gonna hurt you." (I could go on, but I'm certain you've all heard such fake-sounding, empty promises made to horses.) My horse looked at this lady as if she'd bumped her head. If my horse had been a dog, I'm sure she'd have tilted her head and given the woman that "What the …?" look.

After she eventually reached the horse, the lady then began struggling with the halter. It was clear she had no idea how to place it on the the horse's head. I kept quiet. I didn't say a word. I needed this lady to realize how lost she was. She needed to know exactly where she was in her horsemanship journey. So, I let her struggle. I knew the woman was very intelligent because she was a head nurse at a good-sized hospital in East Texas. I also knew that my horse would be patient and wait for this lady to either figure it out or ask for help. She *didn't* ask for help in haltering the mare, which told me volumes about the lady's independence and determination. Eventually she succeeded in getting the halter on the horse correctly, and despite it taking several minutes, I still rewarded her with a compliment and asked her to lead the mare to the grooming area.

This phase didn't go much better. Already I knew the type of horse this lady would need, but we went on with the evaluation exercises. Throughout the grooming, and eventually the round pen exercises, nothing improved. Her skill level was practically zilch. There was nothing wrong with that; we all have to start somewhere, and to her credit, she acknowledged that she was a raw beginner.

The woman very much enjoyed her day with the basics and scheduled a few more sessions to come out and work with my horses, doing very simple groundwork exercises. Her improvements were significant, but she had a long way to go before it would be time for her to actually purchase a horse. Again, to her credit, she seemed to acknowledge as much.

One evening, after a long day of riding, I got a phone call. On the other end of the line was my nurse client, enthusiastically telling me that her husband just bought and set up a round pen at their house and that they were on their way to pick up the eight-year-old gelding that had been gifted to her by a coworker at the hospital. I was excited for her on one hand…and horrified on the other. Although this determined woman had made significant measurable improvements in a few basic horsemanship sessions, she was not ready for a horse of her own yet…in my opinion. However, I admit, I was not surprised by her decision.

A few weeks passed before I received another call from my nurse client. This time her tone had lost its enthusiasm and had been replaced with obvious frustration and disappointment. After she explained the situation, it was determined that it would be best for both her and her horse to come to my facility and work through their issues.

On her first visit to the ranch with her horse, it was apparent as to why my client was frustrated. The horse was lazy, belligerent, non-responsive, and disrespectful with her. After noticing measurable improvements in my client over a few sessions, I asked the woman to what she attributed her successes. She accurately listed the things we had worked on, which were basically applying sound skills to the tasks of becoming a stronger, more assertive leader for her horse. Again, this lady was a head nurse at a large hospital…I was certain one does not rise to that level of responsibility and accountability by being anything less than a good leader.

During her horsemanship lessons, I began to peel back the layers. I merely helped this lady focus on what she wanted to achieve. If you recall, she'd said she wanted some stress relief from the pressures of her job and from the difficulties at home. My questions were (although I had not yet asked them): What was the cause of the stresses in both venues? What were her challenges at her job? What was difficult about her teenaged son? As it turned out, the issues she was experiencing with her son mirrored almost exactly the problems she experienced with her horse. He was lazy, belligerent, non-responsive, and disrespectful. So by learning solid horsemanship, she rediscovered the tools that she already possessed in order to be less stressed at her job and to be more successful in her relationship with her son. The horsemanship helped tremendously with her "humanship." She learned to break things down, make the tasks that she needed done or needed help doing seem as significant to others as they were to her. She learned to be firm but fair. She learned to be assertive. She learned to release and praise with good timing. My client already knew these things, but the horse afforded her an opportunity to practice. As she practiced, she received in return immediate honest feed back from her horse.

The results were not only a better, more responsive, well-behaved, respectful, and safer horse but also a tremendous feeling of satisfaction and self-confidence for my client. Most importantly, the experience during those weeks helped her eventually fulfill her original goal—to feel like that carefree young girl again, working her grandfather's horse.

In the end, I did little more than peel layers and "bend" my client. I "flexed" her. I helped her learn to focus more on the specifics of what seemed like a bigger problem. Ultimately, that which she wanted—to be "straight"—was there all along.

Approximately three years later, my wife and I were having supper at a popular fried catfish restaurant down by Lake Fork. A tall gentleman approached our table and introduced himself. He was the husband of my nurse client. With a hint of a tear in his eye and a shaky voice he thanked me. He went on to explain that the things she had learned from the horsemanship sessions had completely changed their household for the good. The relationships within the family had vastly improved and their once troubled son had become grateful, respectful, and helpful and would soon be heading off to college. He said all this as he shook my hand with vigor and pointed toward the exit door of the restaurant. Standing there with her arm around a nearly grown young man was the nurse lady. She smiled across the room and silently mouthed, "Thank you."

As the nurse's husband walked away, I buried my face in my napkin and fought back my own tears. I was reminded once again to be grateful to God for affording me the opportunity to do what I do. My job is to help people, even if I have to *bend 'em to keep 'em straight*.

CHAPTER 11

THE HORSE IS ALWAYS RIGHT

IT WAS A long drive from Kamloops, Canada, to Sulphur Springs, Texas. Fortunately, I had friends and acquaintances along the way to break up the trip into manageable pieces—for me and the young stud colt traveling with me. My plan was to reverse the trip I had made getting to Kamloops. I had been there giving horsemanship clinics. It was beautiful country, and I greatly appreciated the opportunity to experience it, but it was time to get home.

Our first stop was just outside of Helena, Montana. I had arranged for a couple of days with Curt and Tammy Pate and their children Mesa and Rial. It was close to the Fourth of July, and they were gracious enough to ask me to stay with them and celebrate our country's Independence Day with their family. From there I made another stop in Livingston, Montana, where I gave a private clinic to a couple and one of their guests. It was my last obligation before heading home.

I traveled through the rest of Montana, turned south, and made my way through most of Wyoming to the Cheyenne rodeo grounds. There I turned my traveling partner out in a big area, hooked up my living quarters trailer to water and electricity, and got ready for a good night's rest before continuing the journey early the next morning.

It was good the see the young stud colt romp and play. I'm sure he had no clue nor care that he was running and playing on one of the United States' great historic rodeo sites, home of "The Daddy of 'em All," Cheyenne Frontier Days. To him it was just a place to run, stretch, and get plenty of fresh air after being cooped up in the trailer for several hours and hundreds of miles.

After ensuring that the colt had plenty to eat and drink, I was bedding myself down for the evening when my cell phone rang. It was a friend and fellow professional horseman that learned I was headed home and would be traveling through Colorado the next day. He explained that Mr. Ray Hunt was doing a horsemanship clinic in Colorado just a short detour off the route I was taking home. He suggested I stop by the clinic and see Mr. Ray and his lovely wife Miss Carolyn.

Mr. Ray Hunt was an icon in the horse industry for decades. He was a friend and student of Mr. Tom Dorrance, another individual considered among the founders of "natural horsemanship." I first learned of Mr. Ray very early in my horsemanship journey. The harder I worked and the more I struggled, the more I sought the experience and wisdom of those who'd gone before me. I sought out the Tom Dorrances and Ray Hunts of the world because, at the time, they were the ones generously and expertly sharing their knowledge with others. Mr. Ray was one of the few that I knew of then that actually traveled the country, conducting clinics and presentations to groups interested in learning what he was teaching. Mr. Ray was quick to give a lot of credit and respect to Mr. Tom. It just seemed that Mr. Tom wasn't as eager to travel and share his knowledge, whereas Mr Ray was.

The next morning, my mind was made up—I was determined to take advantage of the opportunity to learn more from Mr. Ray. I packed away my hoses and extension cords, got the playful stud colt loaded in the freshly shavings-bedded trailer, and away we went, with the big "Daddy of 'em All" sign in the side rearviews of my Dodge dually. Only a couple of hours later, I pulled up to the address hosting the Ray Hunt clinic, and one would have thought I was pulling into a small county fair. I was amazed at the number of vehicles and trailers already around the arena area. I parked my rig, unloaded the young stud, tied him to the trailer, and headed out to find where to check in as an auditor of the clinic.

Prior to that day, I'd talked to Mr. Ray only a few times but never attended one of his clinics. I was overwhelmed by the attendance. There were, in my opinion, entirely too many participants on horseback, even though Mr. Ray was doing his best to address them all. I eased around from place to place in search of an area in which I could see and hear better. Along the way I spotted

Miss Carolyn, Mr. Ray's beautiful wife. To be polite I gave her my respects, then walked over closer to the arena so I could hear what Ray was saying.

Well, Mr. Ray spotted me and came over and asked if I could help him. I thought, *What in the world does he need help with? He's obviously got this clinic thing figured out. There's standing room only.* I assumed he wanted me to run an errand or something because he barely knew me.

As it turned out, Mr. Ray had recognized that folks were getting a bit frustrated that they were getting too little attention because he had allowed too many people to take part in the clinic. He needed some help because of the sheer number of riders. There were too many people standing around doing nothing, and he wanted me to keep them involved and answer their questions. I was deeply honored to be able to assist him and that he would even ask. I somehow knew, too, that he wasn't going to pay me a dime to help him. But I was more than happy to volunteer.

Mr. Ray didn't speak to me much during the clinic. At times I felt as if he was bothered that he asked me to help by keeping folks busy and either answering or relaying questions for him. But it seemed like it was a success in the end. Several minutes after the clinic wrapped up, he approached and somewhat harshly asked if I'd like to join him and his wife for dinner. Of course, I accepted the invitation.

We arrived at the restaurant and were seated…and the awkwardness was evident. There was so much I wanted to ask him; however, I just didn't feel comfortable and was afraid to say much. I was uncharacteristically without conversation. For those who know me, I'm sure you're thinking you wish you could have witnessed such an anomaly—Van Hargis, actually sitting quietly and not speaking! Nonetheless, this was the case. Miss Carolyn and I exchanged a few brief words, but Mr. Ray remained fairly silent, only interjecting tidbits here and there.

After a while, out of the clear blue, Mr. Ray sort of cut into his steak in a manner that got my attention. When he finished cutting off a bite, he raised his fork with the fresh piece of meat firmly stuck on the tines and somewhat shook it toward me as if it were a substitute for shaking his finger, and he said somewhat firmly, "The horse is always right."

Shocked a bit by the break in silence, Mr. Ray's mannerisms, and his choice of words, I sat confused, chewing the steak in my mouth slowly and deliberately. Afraid to say anything, I nodded out of respect to let him know I heard his words. I hoped to appear as if I was chewing on what he'd said. And I was. However, to be completely honest there was a part of me that chuckled at the idea of *the horse is always right*.

Ha! I thought. *You've obviously not worked with some of the piece-of-crap horses I've had to start.*

I prayed to God Mr. Ray couldn't read my thoughts.

I also recalled that I'd heard something similar to those words earlier in the day at the clinic. He'd said, "The horse is never wrong." I wondered for a moment if both quotes truly meant the same thing.

Then, there was that change in Mr. Ray again. He abruptly stabbed his steak, sawed off another bite, raised his fork with the meat secure on the tines that he shook toward me, and said, "The horse is always right because he's either doing what comes natural to him or he's doing what he thinks you want him to do. Either way, he's right."

Then into his mouth went the piece of meat, he pulled it from the fork prongs with his teeth, and chewed with vigor. Though he wasn't looking at me, his overall body language seemed to say, "And that's that."

Even though I wasn't paid monetarily for helping Mr. Ray that day, I received a nugget of wisdom that has positively influenced my thinking about horses, horsemanship, and more. What an absolute blessing to have been at the right place at the right time to receive the right message.

The next day I had plenty of time, about thirteen hours, to think about it as I drove from Colorado to Sulphur Springs, Texas. I knew Mr. Ray was exactly right. We can't blame a horse for doing what comes naturally. Additionally, if the horse is doing what he thinks we want him to do, then the burden is on us to be better communicators. If the horse makes a mistake, it is an honest one and likely because we're not properly communicating what we want the horse to do. Perhaps we are not setting up the horse to be successful. *The horse is always right.* I've thought about those words far beyond those thirteen hours. If I don't like a horse's natural behavior, it's up to me to change it. If the horse is not doing what I am asking, then I must realize he's doing what he thinks I want from him. Either way, darn it, the burden is on me.

Since that supper with Mr. Ray, I've observed hundreds and hundreds more horses in various forms and stages of training. I can say without a doubt, when studied with complete objectivity, *the horse is always right.*

Most of my horsemanship career has been spent in two primary areas, although media sources billed me as "one of the most versatile horsemen in the industry." (I'm not sure where that particular claim came from, but I'm honored that they thought so.) Folks tend to want to know in what a horseman "specializes." Perhaps in an effort to satisfy others I should have picked one specialty, but to be honest, I was so drawn to just figuring out horses in general, I failed to do so. Still, it seems to me that two areas seemed to keep me the busiest: colt-starting and ranch horse versatility.

Mr. Ray's statement about the horse always being right was one of those points that inspired my study. I've heard a number of my horsemanship mentors refer to themselves as "students of the horse." The ones who seemed to have the greatest understanding of the horse appeared to be the ones that worked the hardest—not at acquiring trophies, buckles, or titles, but at finding ways to get along better with the horse and share that with others. Heck, there must be something good for the mind, body, and soul to do so, too. Three out of four of the greatest horsemen of our time lived to be in their late eighties to mid-nineties, and the fourth—one of my heroes, Mr. Jack Brainard—left this earth at the age of one hundred. He inspired me to frequently say, "I have no desire to retire." I may not be able to ride many horses when I'm ninety-nine, but God willing, I may still be able to help others get along with them.

I digress. Back to my specialty…I don't have one. My journey has been to learn as much as I can from the great horsemen and from the greatest horsemanship teacher there is—the horse. If we are humble enough to listen and know, without a doubt, that the horse is just trying to survive the moment the best, most comfortable, and most efficient way he can, then there's very little that cannot be achieved in the human/horse relationship. If we know, without a doubt, that every bit of feedback the horse gives us is one hundred percent honest with no ulterior motives other than just to "get along," then we know that to achieve whatever it is we want to achieve with a horse depends on our ability to communicate our ideas to him.

How does that work with everything else we do from a training perspective? First of all, it is very reassuring to know that the horse is going to give sound, honest feedback to everything we ask of him. It is humbling to know that the horse likely is better at training us than we are at training him. I've given in to that to a certain degree. When asked what I am going to do in training a particular horse, I frequently respond, "I don't know. I have to wait until the horse tells me what he needs."

Many years ago, likely in late 1991 or early '92, when asked by a local newspaper about my "horsemanship methods," my response came without hesitation. I said, "I train from the horse's perspective." Which I suppose is just another way of saying I practice "natural horsemanship." In studying the horse, we know some things are as close to absolute as absolute can be. Such as, we know that horses are flight animals. We know they are bigger, stronger, and swifter than we are. We know that because horses have big bodies and fast metabolisms, they desire to be efficient in all they do. This means that in order to get a desired response or behavior from the horse, we simply must ask the right question in a way that aligns with these natural characteristics. We will know immediately if our idea or approach is on the right track because the horse will give us one hundred percent honest feedback, naturally.

Even though "natural horsemanship" is a very popular phrase, there's nothing natural about the horse and human relationship from the horse's perspective. It's very demanding on the horse. However, it's our duty and obligation to the horse and to ourselves to modify the horse's natural behavior to a degree, so that the horse can get along with us, be productive, and be safe in the situations and circumstances in which we place him in our human world. When I stop and think about the mistakes horses make, I know I can live with and correct those mistakes—those *honest* mistakes—simply by being simpler and more thorough in setting the horse up to be successful.

Mr. Ray's quote helped me take a closer look at myself and my communication skills. The key is to try to see things from the horse's perspective, to break things down in such a simple way he just can't help but be correct in what we ask of him (which I talk about in chapter 5—p. 38).

The horse is always right. He's either doing what comes naturally or he's doing what he thinks we want him to do. When I think about these sentences, they really have little to do with the horse. The horse is just the mirror of whatever it is *we* are trying to achieve. We have to come up with a plan that is simple to follow and achievable. This brings us once again to my four questions of successful horsemanship and "humanship": 1) What do you want? 2) Is what you want achievable? 3) Can you communicate what you want in a way that can be understood? 4) Can the result be measured?

Trust in these questions, have faith in your process, and know without a shadow of a doubt that *the horse is always right.*

CHAPTER 12

TATERS, EGGS, OR TEA BAGS?

As you learned in the first chapter of this book, when I lived in Sulphur Springs, Texas, I went to a small church called The Gathering. The pastor was the great guy I've mentioned before, Brother Kris Childress. He often had great stories to go along with his sermons and shared them with such passion that it was practically impossible not to be positively affected by them.

One morning he shared a story about how we are all affected by challenges that come along on our life's journey.

"Would you rather be a potato, an egg, or a tea bag?" Brother Kris asked. He then paused for several seconds. At first, I chuckled, then questioned if I'd heard him correctly. He repeated, "Think about it. Would you rather be a potato, an egg, or a tea bag?"

Yup, I thought. *I heard him correctly.* Then I thought, *Man, I'm just as lost as a ball in hide weeds.*

Finally, the pastor went on with his story, describing a pot of boiling water. "That's life," he explained. "Sometimes life is turbulent and uncomfortable."

Brother Kris went on to say that if you looked at life from the standpoint of a potato and you got thrown into a pot of boiling water (that is, bad things can happen, and they will), how would that affect you? You'd get all soft and mushy. Now, if you are an egg and get thrown into a pot of boiling water, you will get hard. In fact, the longer you are in there, the harder you get and the tougher you become. However, when you are a tea bag thrown into a pot of boiling water, the bad things (hot, turbulent, uncomfortable) don't have an effect on you, you have an effect on them.

The point of the story was, we have choices in how our life experiences affect us. We get to choose what we want to take from those circumstances.

As Brother Kris continued sharing his sermon with the congregation, I felt myself drifting back in my memory as I recalled a specific day and all the details of it, as if I were reliving it. The pastor's voice seemed to get more and more faint as I recalled more and more details from the past. It was as if, while sitting on that padded wooden church pew, I was having a dream. But it was no dream; it was the memory of a very distinct and important moment in my life.

Like a lot of teenaged kids, I had a high school romance. My girlfriend Cindy and I were the couple in high school that everyone either loved and adored or hated and envied. We were a couple for most of our high school years. I was "Joe Jock" and she was the head cheerleader. We were both good students bound for college and seemed to have it made. Heck, our senior year we were even voted "Mr. & Miss CHS" (Commerce High School).

Cindy's dad owned a successful automobile repair business in Commerce, Texas, and was in need of a car part that wasn't available locally. Cindy and I volunteered to make the short thirty-minute drive to get the needed part from a store in Greenville. As we were driving along, chatting, and most likely listening to radio tunes popular in the late seventies, Cindy spoke up and said, "Look, there's your old house."

"Yup," I replied after a pause. "That's my old house."

It is hard to describe the emotions that swept through me each time I drove past my stepfather's place…my old house. There were so many great memories there. Heck, it was the place of my childhood. Tragically, though, for every good memory there were horrific ones involving abuse. At almost every point on the property I could tell you where a violent argument or beating occurred, involving my mother and stepfather. I could certainly tell you where I had been whipped, hit, or kicked. But nobody knew it. My mother and I were experts at hiding what we felt were disgraceful secrets.

When Cindy said, "Look, there's your old house," she justifiably assumed that because it was the residence of my youth, that I had wonderful memories of it. She did not know the "rest of the story." She knew me, though.

And I knew she noticed that whenever we drove past the place, I got quiet for a mile or two.

However, on this particular day, I didn't just get quiet. I suddenly stepped hard on the brake because we were almost to the driveway. My sudden movement and the excessively fast deceleration of the car surprised Cindy, and she put both hands on the dash and shouted, "What's wrong?" We weren't quite slowed down enough, but I turned into the diamond-shaped drive anyway. Undoubtedly upset by our change of speed, direction, and plans, she exclaimed, "What in the world are we doing?"

After the vehicle had come to a complete stop, we sat there without speaking for a moment. I could feel Cindy staring at me as she quartered her body slightly toward me with her right hand still on the dash of the car. Both my hands were on the steering wheel as I stared at the instruments panel.

Finally, I broke the silence, turning to look at Cindy with tears building in my eyes as I said, "I'm just so tired of hating him. I'm tired of him being in my mind all the time. Every minute of every day, he's there." By now the tears were too many and too heavy to be contained, and they rolled—they rolled and they rolled. Cindy didn't even understand who I hated or why I hated him. She was a smart girl, though, and was quickly putting pieces of the puzzle together.

I turned to open my car door and started to step out. "I'll be right back," I said over my shoulder.

As the door closed, I heard Cindy say, "What are you doing?"

I knew where my stepfather would be. I walked with a purpose toward the gate between the house and the barn area. As I made my way through the gate, I purposefully rattled its chain in hopes he would hear it. I turned toward the barn and began to walk as if I was walking out on a football field—my domain! I was not going to let him win this battle!

Just as I passed the horse walker on my way by the horse barn, my stepfather appeared from around the corner. I stopped. My fists clenched. He walked toward me with a smile on his face and said, "Hey son, I knew you'd come back."

I wiped my runny nose and rubbed away what was left of my tears. "Stop right there you son of a bitch, I'm not back!" I shouted. Then…I'll never forget the words that came from my mouth. They flowed as if I'd rehearsed them a thousand times. "I'm sick and tired of hating you. Not a full minute goes by without a thought or a memory of you, and it's never good. I can't live the rest of my life with this much hate for you. It's hurting me inside. *I have to forgive you.*" And then, "I forgive you!"

I paused just for a moment so I could soak up the shocked expression on his face. Then I turned and walked away before he could say anything. As I'd walked in, I walked out of that yard as tall and as proud as I could. It was easier on the way out. A burden had been lifted off my shoulders and from my heart. I heard his voice behind me, but I had no idea what he was saying. It no longer mattered.

When I opened the car door and sat down, it was as if I was sitting an inch off the seat. Cindy asked what had happened, and all I said was, "I forgave him."

Soon, the reality of the moment set in. I quickly learned that forgiveness is not a thing you do one time. It is a process. It's a very long process. Part of my process was to make something better from the bad and be grateful. From my twelve years of hell on earth with my stepfather, I was grateful for learning about the horseman that I didn't want to be, the husband I didn't want to be, the father I didn't want to be, and the man I didn't want to be. From Brother Kris' message that morning, I was reminded that my years in the pot of boiling water transitioned me from fear to hate, from hate to forgiveness, from forgiveness to gratitude.

I chose the tea bag.

There can be many boiling points in life. One year before school started after summer break, we made plans to take the girls to Six Flags Over Texas in Arlington. We were getting an early start. As my wife was busy getting the last of our stuff and the girls in the truck, I made a final pass through the horse barn to make sure everything was safe and secure. All was well and ready. Checked and re-checked.

When I jumped in my truck filled with two excited young girls and a slightly flustered adult, my wife said, "Did you 'Nick-proof' the barn?"

"Yup, all is well," I replied. "The barn is Nick-proofed."

At some point in a horse owner's life, a special horse comes around that's a true character—an absolute blessing and a royal pain in the backside, too. Well, at my ranch, we seem to never be without one of those types. Nick was one that was by far the nicest horse on the place—the best-looking…and the most mischievous. The term "Nick-proof" meant everything on our property had to be latched, double-latched, and safety-latched. Nick had the talent and the patience to open anything at the facility. If he wasn't tied up securely or in a stall, locked up like the Huntsville State Prison, then rest assured, he'd open a gate and have horses and cattle co-mingling and scattered everywhere. So, before we left the property, everything had to be Nick-proofed.

Away we went to spend too much money having too much fun at Six Flags! Hours later we arrived home with two worn-out, theme-parked girls and an empty wallet. It was time to put everyone away in their beds and check the horse barn.

My initial pass through the barn seemed good, but I had an odd feeling. Before leaving for the theme park, Nick was turned out in one of our outdoor pens. I had a sense I should lay eyes on him before retiring for the night. As I approached his turnout pen, I noticed the gate open. Actually, I wasn't surprised, even though I had left it latched and chained. Where the heck was he, though? I scanned the area and couldn't see him. Then I noticed another gate opened. Another gate that had been latched and chained. Now both Nick and Joe were out somewhere. When those two were together, then sure something was going to be jacked up. Under the best of circumstances, those two horses were mischief-makers. Weirdly though, nothing seemed out of place other than the fact that Nick and Joe were nowhere to be found.

I began to feel a little suspicious. I feared that because Nick and Joe had been my demo horses at countless clinics and expos and were well known that perhaps they had been stolen. I checked the front drive-through gate. It was still secured and there was no sign of anyone cutting the chain. I resisted the temptation to worry, but I was perplexed as to where the two Houdinis were hiding. I decided to make one more pass through the barn, as if they'd somehow reappear. I felt like I was looking for a giant set of missing car keys. I kept looking in the same places I'd already checked, as if they would magically show up.

Upon entering the aisleway of the horse barn, I noticed the doorknob to my office—the first door on the right when entering the barn—seemed to have horse nose smudges on it. That was unusual. Doorknobs are usually slick and polished-looking from being used frequently. Confused but curious, I paused for a moment then opened the door.

It was as if I had opened the door to a steam room. A big waft of hot air rushed from the room, and it smelled foul of horse piss and poop. I tried opening the door fully but couldn't. Blocking the door were Joe's hind legs. He was laid out on the floor partially in my office and the adjoining restroom. Shocked by what I was seeing, I could only think, *Where's Nick?* I stepped over Joe in a daze and looked in the bathroom. Sure enough, to the left of the door, there was Nick, slumped and sitting as if he'd been trained to do so. Unlike Joe's eyes, which were flat and dead-looking, Nick appeared to have only just passed. His eyes still looked bright and moist. I jumped fully into the room and quickly laid my ear on Nick's heart-girth area, listening for any sounds of life…a heartbeat, a breath…anything. I placed my fingers under his jaw and prayed for a pulse. I thought about CPR. *Can CPR be done on a horse? I'll try!* I shoved one fist as deep into one of Nick's nostrils as possible…with the other hand, I awkwardly held his lips closed the best I could…then I shoved my face into his other nostril and blew with everything I had. Nothing! *Blow harder!* I thought. I filled my lungs as full as I could get them and blew again for all I was worth. Nothing. *Chest compressions!* I remembered. I rose to my feet and slammed my shoulder into Nick's chest area three times, then dropped to my knees, lowered my ear to his chest, and listened.

I repeated the desperate movements again and again. Blowing and blowing. Slamming, slamming, and slamming. Blowing and blowing.

Nick was dead. The overwhelming Texas August heat and no ventilation was more than the horses could endure.

Until that day I had never experienced the death of anyone or anything I had been that close to. Nick had been my best friend. Some will understand exactly what I mean by that. My older brother died in a car crash when I was barely three, but thankfully, I had been too young to know him or grasp the loss of him. I had not yet experienced grief. Believe me, I've now learned about grieving. Without a doubt, I have experienced all seven stages of grief, although disbelief and acceptance resurface occasionally.

For as long as I can remember, I've felt a presence with me. From the first time I learned of God and Jesus Christ, I knew what that presence was. Did I understand it? No. But I knew it existed. I knew *they* existed. Because of that feeling and that belief, I never doubted that all things happen for a reason. Therefore, I knew that Nick and Joe died that day for a reason. For a very long time I prayed for the reason and the lesson to be revealed to me. Even though I eventually fully accepted the deaths of those two amazing horses, one of which was my best friend, I was still seeking *the why*.

When a year or so had passed since Nick's shoes were pulled from his feet and he was laid to rest under his favorite trees, not far from the pond he frequently splashed around in, my phone rang. It was my grandmother. I could tell by her voice that something wasn't quite right. She asked if I'd come over to help her with something. Our back doors were less than two hundred yards apart. I could see her standing in her back screen door, watching me approach.

As I strode closer, I could see her face more and more clearly. When I stepped on her porch, I could see that my grandmother, the most stoic woman I'd ever known, was visibly upset. Though not a tear could be seen in her eyes, she struggled to say, "I think Allen is dead. Will you check? I can't."

My heart dropped to the floor. Allen Ray Gammill, my grandfather, my closest and most influential positive male role model, was dead.

My question about what seemed like Nick's untimely death was answered. It was perfect. Nick taught me about grieving and how important each phase of grieving was so that I'd be prepared for the most difficult death I'd face thus far in my life.

Thank you, Nick. Even in death you continued to teach me. First you taught me how to get on a path of better horsemanship. You taught me about friendship. You taught me more about humor and mischief. You taught me…

I was tossed in that hot boiling turbulent water. I had a choice to make: taters, eggs, or tea bags? I chose tea bags.

CHAPTER 13

THAT'S MIGHTY FINE DOIN'S

As a child, my grandmother frequently told me about one of her neighbors, Mr. William Chamness, who used to visit on a pretty regular basis. He, of course, was a fellow dairyman. It seemed everyone in the Hopkins County area back in that day and time was in the agricultural industry in one way or another. The banks in town were heavily invested in the agricultural industry. There were milk-, cheese-, and butter-processing plants in town that employed many local citizens. There were trucking businesses that hauled raw milk to the plants and processed products from the plants. There were even companies that disposed of or used the waste materials from the plants. The Sulphur Springs and Hopkins County area was most definitely an agriculture-dependent economy back in those days. Often, folks such as my grandparents were in the dairy business and also ran stocker cattle.

Without a doubt, my grandparents were extremely hard-working people. Their days started very early in the morning, often long before sunrise. They'd both make their way to the dairy barn and prepare the barn and the machinery for milking time. As my grandfather finished preparations, my grandmother would walk through the drip shed, open the gates and start letting the giant-uddered milk cows in to make their way to the flat eight-stall milking parlor. Most of the cows pushed and shoved their way on the grooved concrete toward the opening of the barn to eat and relieve their swollen bags of the milk they'd produced overnight. Meanwhile, my grandmother would walk out in the pasture to gather any stragglers that were perhaps less experienced or less enthused about their twice-a-day routine. My grandmother often said that the walk to gather stragglers was her favorite time of day. She even claimed to enjoy the task when it snowed, which typically is a Texas dairyman's nightmare. Fortunately for them, snow in Hopkins County was a rare occasion. She said she loved how different everything looked with a light blanket of snow on it, and she loved to hear the crunch under her feet.

After her walk around the latecomers, the gate to the drip shed was closed and the real rhythm of milking cattle began. As my grandfather used to say, "There aint never nothin' to do." It seemed like my grandparents worked like a well-oiled machine together. Everything they did was perfectly efficient. Each one knew exactly what the other was doing and not a movement was wasted. The chatter between them was easy, quiet, deliberate, and matter-of-fact. While one was scooping shit, the other was dumping feed. While one was hosing off and cleaning udders and teats, the other was placing on milkers. They were truly amazing to watch and learn from. This routine was smooth and nonstop, from the first cow to the last.

Finally, after the last cow's milk made its way to the tank, it was cleanup time. All the milkers and hoses had to be flushed and sterilized, and the drip shed scraped and hosed. As my grandmother finished the last of the sterilization and made sure the milk tank cooler temperature was perfect, she would slip off toward the house to start breakfast. Meanwhile, my grandfather would finish scraping all the manure from the drip shed and start shoveling shit into the manure spreader. Once all the manure was in the spreader, the drip shed was hosed off until it was completely clean and glistening from water to be ready and clean for the evening milking. I knew when my grandfather was done and could start toward the house for breakfast once he began spraying his rubber boots. My grandfather liked to have his boots clean.

Just as my grandfather arrived on the back porch, my grandmother would be pulling hot fresh biscuits from the oven. All the other breakfast fixings were on the table with places set for the three of us. "Wash up and sit down. Breakfast is ready," she'd say.

Maybe not coincidently, on many occasions, just as my grandfather would slide his chair under the table and place his napkin in his lap, there'd be a knock at the back door and a call out: "Allen? Della Fay?"

"Come in here, Willy," my grandfather would say without even looking up. "You're just in time for breakfast."

"Ah, I'm not gonna bother y'all's breakfast. I'll just have a cup of coffee," Mr. Chamness would say.

"Slide around, boy, and let this man sit down," my grandfather would tell me.

Then my grandmother of course would insist on getting Mr. Chamness a plate and heap it for him with bacon or sausage and farm-fresh eggs. Biscuits were hot, covered with a kitchen towel, and ready for the taking. Butter, syrup, and homemade fruit jelly was on the table.

The visit and hospitality was always accompanied with semi-polite smacking of the lips. To clarify, proper smacking was to let those around you, especially the cook, know just how much you were enjoying the food. Too much smacking was just rude behavior and darned near heathenistic. But just the right amount of smacking, well, that was a compliment to a country woman's cooking. The most experienced breakfast crashers had perfected the proper smacking. Mr. Chamness was a downright artist. He had the whole process down to a science. He knew my grandparents' routine, he knew just the right amount of smacking to do, and he even knew what to chitchat about with my grandfather to rile him up so Mr. Chamness could eat the last biscuit before my grandfather could get to it. I'm telling you…he was brilliant at breakfast-crashing.

All joking aside, Mr. Chamness was a hard worker and well-respected fellow rancher and dairyman, as well as a good friend and neighbor. My grandparents enjoyed having him over, and I did too. He was a cheerful sort and always when they got through eating, he would compliment my grandmother in a way that was both flattering to her cooking and humorously memorable, too. He'd push away from the table a bit, wipe his face one last time with his napkin, lean back in his chair, rub his belly, and say, "Ms. Della, that was mighty fine doin's."

Several years passed, my grandparents got out of the dairy business, and Mr. Chamness didn't visit as frequently. But his saying "mighty fine doin's" stuck around our household. Anytime someone said or did anything of significance my grandmother would say, "Well, that was mighty fine doin's." Occasionally, she'd then share a story or two about Mr. Chamness and his breakfast visits, and she'd always credit him for his country compliment—although my grandmother popularized that quote probably more so than he did.

Through the years, that quote has remained on the tip of my tongue. Perhaps partly in appreciation of the fact that Mr. Chamness was always a good friend to the family and very appreciative of the meals he shared with us. There're many different ways to say "thank you" or "job well done." I've always thought this quote was a good way to do it. It's become another way for me to express gratitude and appreciation for what we have in our lives. That's one of the greatest lessons I try to tell people. Whenever we're working with horses or spending time with people in our daily lives, always take a moment to be grateful and appreciative for what we have and for what others have done for us.

Many times in my riding lessons, clinics, or even during demonstrations at horse fairs or expos, I'll stop people dead square in what they are doing and tell them they did something positive. They may not even be aware of what they did. I want to compliment them nonetheless. Oftentimes they might feel anxious because of what the horse is doing or not doing. They could be anxious about what they think the horse *might* do. Regardless, in the midst of an anxious moment, it can be good to hear a compliment. Hopefully, they'll not only accept it, but maybe, just maybe, they'll give their horse a rub and pass the compliment on. So, I make it a point sometimes to yell out to my students, "As my grandmother would say, 'That's mighty fine doin's!'"

I've had more than a few people ask me over the years, "What does that mean?" Of course, that gives me the opportunity to tell them the story of the quote and talk about my grandmother, her breakfasts, and a dear friend that used to appreciate her cooking.

I have to remind myself that it's not just about rewarding and therefore motivating people in their daily lives, but when I'm riding my horses, I have to be keenly aware what it is I'm looking for so I can quickly reward *them*.

If we understand how horses learn—through the release of any sort of pressure—we realize, then, from their perspective, they are trying hard to please us so they can be relieved of whatever pressure they are experiencing from us. What that means to us is we need to always be looking for something positive in their actions or behavior. It is important to focus on not what the horse doing wrong, but the effort being put toward getting it right. Look for those moments to pause, rub the horse on the neck, pat him on the butt, and say to the horse, "Good job. That's mighty fine doin's."

Of course, I'm not so sure horses know what I'm saying, but I do have a very strong feeling that they know that quote is a positive thing. I'm very much a believer that horses feel our emotions. It's been proven to me in too many cases. I think when we go out there and work with a horse expecting the best, we'll often get the best from him. It's amazing to me that some of the best horsemen I know are some of the most positive people I know. The same thing went for my coaches in high school and college. Some of the best coaches I played for were also very positive people. Even though they weren't afraid to correct us when we did something wrong, they were quicker to reward us when we did something well. *That's* what they were looking for. Because they were looking for good, they were quick to see it.

We tend to get what we are looking for. Therefore, look for the positive in a horse's behavior, and you'll be quicker to see it. Then reward it. Look for the positive in others, and you'll be quick to see it. Then reward it.

As Mr. Willam Chamness figured out to an artful science, show up at the right time, smack a little but not too much, lean back and say with conviction, "That's mighty fine doin's."

I dedicate this chapter to my grandmother Della Fay Gammill (1919–2015).

REWARD THE THOUGHT

WHILE UNSADDLING A two-year-old colt in the hallway of my modest horse barn, I heard from the house, "You're gonna want to take this call."

"Who is it?" I called back.

"It's Mr. Brainard, Jack Brainard," was the reply.

I secured that colt as fast as I could and practically sprinted toward the house. I could count on one finger the number of times my hero, Mr. Jack Brainard, had reached out to contact me. With each quick step toward the house I guessed as to what he had to tell me or ask me. As I answered the phone, I made an effort not to sound out of breath from both the sprint and the excitement.

Mr. Jack asked what I was doing the coming weekend. Before I could answer my imagination was running wild. I was thinking he might want me to come ride a colt for him or help him out with a difficult horse or…. My heart was racing but before I could answer he followed up by saying, "Tom Dorrance is going to be at my place for a few days."

My heart was really racing now. For a moment I imagined I was getting a personal invitation to hang out with two of the greatest horsemen of our time. Two horsemanship icons. Two horsemanship legends.

"You need to be at my place this weekend. We are hosting a clinic that you need to attend," he continued in his characteristically soft tone. "This will be the first and likely the last clinic Tom will do in Texas. All the riding spots are taken, but there's still plenty of room for more auditors."

I was still excited but admittedly a little deflated. I liked what I had imagined better. There for a moment, I'd thought I ranked high enough on Mr. Jack's

VIP list that I was getting a special invitation to be a personal guest. Instead I had to settle for just an invite to be a paying auditor at the clinic. However, this wasn't just any clinic. This was a Tom Dorrance clinic in Texas, only two hours' drive from my house. I promptly told Mr. Jack that I'd change whatever plans happened to be on my schedule, and I would be at the clinic.

When I pulled through the gate at Mr. Jack's place, the Diamond B in Aubrey, there was a vehicle parked in just about every conceivable space you could park one. It was amazing how many folks were there to see Mr. Jack and Mr. Tom. While walking toward the office to register as an auditor, I recognized nearly every face I saw. The Aubrey/Pilot Point area of North Texas was, and to some degree still is, considered the horse capitol of Texas, if not the United States. The area has a great climate. It has good ground for both riding horses and producing grass and hay. It also has easy access to major highways to get to the bigger horse shows, and lastly, it is in close proximity to high-paying jobs, which means clients with disposable income to spend on horses.

Most of the top performance horse trainers lived close to this region and the surrounding areas. As a result, the attendance at the clinic was like going to a Who's Who in the horse business. Mr. Jack had his large riding arena cleverly divided off to provide a big enough space to accommodate approximately fifteen riders. There was also a small oval pen for a colt-starting presentation. Additionally, there was an area with chairs in rows for the auditors wishing to sit and ample space for folks wishing to stand without blocking the view of those in chairs. Lastly, and perhaps most importantly, there was a raised platform strategically located so Mr. Jack and Mr. Tom could see each designated area and be seen and heard by riders and auditors.

When Mr. Tom finally started his way toward his elevated speaking area, I was excited to see him but simultaneously quite taken back by his frailty. In my mind the man was larger than life, yet here before me was a fragile little man, clumsily struggling to make his way through the crowd over the loose uneven surface of the arena floor. To make the short walk from his golf cart even more challenging, Mr. Tom had to support himself in part with crutches. But once Mr. Tom was seated comfortably in his chair on the speaker's platform, introduced by Mr. Jack, and handed a microphone, his soft-spoken voice could be clearly heard throughout the arena and clinic area. Mr. Tom quickly reassured us that even though time had worn on his body, his humor was spared. He shared a few entertaining stories, then went on to explain why we were all there. Not because of him, he said, but because of the horse.

As a professional horseman, I hung on every word he said. I wanted to learn. Throughout the clinic, one could tell that Mr. Tom's focus was to encourage folks to see things through the horse's eyes and practice getting in touch with the horse's mind through his feet. He consistently encouraged riders in the arena to do certain exercises in an effort to help them "feel" their horses' feet, rhythm, and balance.

It seemed that time sped by too quickly. At the end of the day, I took a moment to say thank you to Mr. Jack for calling to inform me of the clinic. While briefly speaking with him, I noticed Mr. Tom and his lovely wife Miss Margaret sitting at a table, selling his book *True Unity*. I excused myself and approached the table. I was about to introduce myself when Mr. Tom said, "Well, hello, Van. Thank you for coming today." I was floored that he knew my name. (I'd notice later on that he knew quite a few trainers' names. I guessed that he read a lot of horse industry magazines and journals.)

After a brief conversation, I bought Mr. Tom's book and asked if he'd please sign it. He was about to do so when I interrupted him to make a special request. "Mr. Tom, I'd like you to sign my book, but I'd also appreciate if you'd write a few words of wisdom you think would be helpful to an aspiring horseman like me."

He stopped, paused, and explained that it had been a long day, and to come up with a few meaningful words, he'd have to give it some thought. He asked if I was coming back the next day.

"Of course," I replied. He closed the book, handed it to me, and promised he'd write something in it tomorrow. Elated to say the least, it seemed like I walked on air all the way to my truck.

The next day the crowd was just as large, but I was fortunate enough to get a seat almost in the same spot as the previous day. The focus was on colt-starting. Two very fresh colts from West Texas, brought by long-time friend Tim Spivey, were to be handled, saddled, and ridden in the oval pen. Did I say these colts were fresh? For those that might not have a grasp on what a cowboy means by "fresh" in this context, it means those suckers were as wild as March hares. Just in case *that* doesn't clear it up, it means that they were raised up to that point in big ranch country, driven up to the working pens on horseback, run into a chute, and until they were mugged in the chute to get a halter on them, they'd not been touched by a human hand. They were "fresh." They'd still kick, paw, bite, and run over you. But they had halters on 'em now.

(Sadly, some folks would claim those colts were already halter-broke because they had halters on. I learned decades ago, everybody's definition of "broke" is different.)

The goal for the day was to demonstrate to and teach everyone at the clinic steps and means to getting a horse from that fresh to (hopefully) being ridden quietly and safely for both handler and horse. The students in the round pen with the horses were Tim Spivey's sons, both teenaged cowboys. They were assisted in part by Tim and one of Mr. Jack's ranch hands.

I was particularly interested in watching how Mr. Tom would instruct the young men.

The majority of my business at that point in my career was starting colts for big ranch outfits, breeders, and several individual clients in East Texas. However, a growing part of my business was starting cutting and reining futurity prospects for many of the trainers I had noted were in the audience at the clinic. I was glad they saw me there, trying to learn more. It would surely help their confidence in my abilities.

What I did learn as I listened to everything Mr. Tom shared was the absolute importance of timing. Timing was critical. I'll take this moment to remind you of a previous chapter: Where You Release Is What You Teach (see p. 45). In that chapter I emphasized how a horse learns— through the release of pressure. Understanding how a horse learns, clearly knowing what you want the horse to do, and having good timing will give you remarkable results. That is *if* consistency, persistence, and faith in your process is practiced.

Even though Mr. Tom was not in the oval pen with the colts, one could see his undeniable and full understanding of the horses. He knew what they needed. He knew how to help them learn to trust, relax, and figure out their new world with humans. I've frequently told folks that in order to be a good horseman, you must know how to read a horse well enough to know what he is about to do *before* he does it. Understanding the horse, combined very delicately with perfect timing, while simultaneously staying firmly grounded in the moment is what it's like to have "feel" in horsemanship. It is not natural. It is learned, practiced, and never fully obtained. Without a doubt, Mr. Tom had "feel." The evidence was in his timing. Again, keep in mind, it was not him in the pen with the horses, which meant his understanding and timing had to be such that he could read the horse, assess what needed to be done, and communicate that in a way and in time for the young men in the arena to do what needed to be done so the horse would get the proper help at the exact proper moment. Whew! I hope y'all followed that. I'm not sure I could write that again.

I've told the story about Mr. Tom working through those young men to help those horses a thousand times but…goodness, it was something to see, and I'm grateful to have witnessed it.

The point is, Mr. Tom's timing was perfect. To those that had not started many colts, I'm sure they were only mildly impressed by witnessing what took place. But, to those of us with careers as horse trainers, and especially those who started colts, we witnessed mastery. By the end of that day both "fresh" colts were relaxed, saddled, mounted, and ridden without incident.

As soon as the clinic ended that day, Mr. Tom again made his way to his book table and sat beside Miss Margaret. He was visibly tired. Out of respect for his fatigue, I hesitated to approach him. But selfishly, I wanted his words of wisdom in my book. When I reached the table, his eyes met mine, and at first, he greeted me as if I were a new face. Then he recognized me and said, "Ah well, Van, you see, after I ate dinner last night, I was too tired to do much thinkin'. I didn't think of anything good to write in your book. Are you coming back tomorrow?"

"Not a problem Mr. Dorrance. I'll be here again tomorrow. I'll see you then, sir." I was a tad bit disappointed, but his weariness was understandable given that fact that he was at least eighty-six and had been talking for two days straight. Although, considering how clever he was, I thought for moment that perhaps he was just training me to come back all three days by recognizing how badly I wanted him to write something in my book.

On the third day, it was evident Mr. Tom was very tired. His speech was a little slower and his wit wasn't quite as sharp. Oh, he still said a few funny things, like, "The parrot will keep squawking 'til you give it a cracker," a remark he made if he had to repeat himself several times in an effort to get people to finally do what he was asking of them. For example, when trying to get a lady to ask her horse to move his hips he said, "Now, move your leg back."…"Move your leg back."…"Try moving your leg back."…"Move your leg back."…"The parrot will keep squawking 'til you give it a cracker." It was funny when he said such things because his tone wouldn't change nor would his inflection. The icing on the cake was when whomever he was speaking to actually did what he was asking—the crowd would laugh and Mr. Tom would clap with delight one time, smile, and say, "Got a cracker."

I'm quite certain I could have listened to Mr. Tom for several more hours, but for his sake, I was glad when the clinic was over. With hope and fingers crossed, I once again approached his book-signing table. I no sooner opened the book to the page I wanted him to sign when he looked at me, reached to his shirt pocket, pulled out a piece of paper, and said, "Van, I'm happy you came back today. I thought of something you might like." He took my book, unfolded the piece of paper from his pocket, and with his bent-up, aged fingers, slowly and carefully copied three words from the paper. I couldn't quite make out what he wrote from where I stood, and as soon as he signed his name, he closed the book and told me to wait until I had time to think about it before I read what he wrote. I shook his hand lightly, but firm enough to show my respects, carefully placed the book under my arm, and walked away one hundred percent satisfied from the three-day experience at the Diamond B.

Mr. Tom had told me to wait until I had time to think about it before I read what he wrote, but by the time I got to Highway 380 and headed east toward home, I could wait no longer. After all, Sulphur Spring was still another hour and a half away. "That's plenty of time to think," I justified. The book, *True Unity*, was sitting there on the edge of the bench seat just behind the stick shift in my Chevy truck. I checked the traffic ahead carefully. There were no cars for a while and no intersections coming up so I flipped the book cover open and read the three words Mr. Tom had written. I quickly shut the book and stared straight through my bug-soiled windshield. *What the hell?* I thought. I contemplated turning my truck around to ask him what he meant by those three words. I'd hung on every word he'd said during the clinic, and not once in three days had I heard him say what was written in my book.

I drove and I thought. I thought a lot. I thought about *Reward the thought.*

Weeks passed since meeting Tom Dorrance and learning from his horsemanship clinic at Mr. Jack's place. Each time I worked or rode a horse, I thought about the clinic, his book, and those three words. I thought about his discussing "feel," timing, and balance. Each time I started a new two-year-old under saddle, I recalled listening to Mr. Tom coaching Tim's boys on how to transition those "fresh" colts to quiet and confident horses. He did it by reading both the horses and the boys perfectly. I thought a lot about being a better horseman.

From the time I was a small child I was told by family members, teachers, and coaches that I was a natural athlete. As I got older they'd comment on my hand-eye coordination, timing, balance, and speed. I suppose awareness of those characteristics helped me develop them into useful tools toward becoming successful at sports. But hand-eye coordination, timing, balance, and speed still is only enough to be a *good* athlete. One athletic trait that in my opinion is commonly overlooked is *awareness*. More specifically, *situational awareness*. A *great* athlete has keen situational awareness in addition to the aforementioned traits. If you're a sports fan, at some point you've either seen or heard of someone speak of an athlete that always seems to be around the ball or always seems to be in the right place at the right time. One might say that athlete has a "feel" for the game. How does one "feel" such a thing? My argument is you don't. I categorize "feel" as situational awareness. It's a skill. Like all skills, it too can be developed and enhanced through practice and hard work. I'd wager that every parent, teacher, or coach at some point has encouraged a child to "pay attention." In other words, be aware, present, and focused.

Perhaps genetics helped with a few of the traits folks seemed to credit as natural athleticism. I'm not going to argue that point here. However, I will argue that, in my opinion, *my* situational awareness skills, my ability to pay attention, was developed and enhanced considerably for twelve years during that formidable time in my life when our household was violent and abusive. One learns survival skills when in situations where one's safety is in frequent potential danger. Please don't think for a moment that I'm saying all good or great athletes were or even may have been raised in abusive households. I'm merely confident in saying that my situational awareness skills were likely heightened by the abusive experiences of my youth. Situational awareness was not something I can remember consciously practicing. Thankfully, though, I developed it. Without a doubt, it kept me safer as a child. And it likely played an important role in my high school and college athletic ability.

Tom Dorrance displayed unbelievably keen situational awareness when he helped Tim's boys get those "fresh" colts started under saddle without incident. Remember how I said Mr. Tom's understanding and timing had to be such that he had to read the horse, assess what needed to be done, communicate that in a way and in time for the young men in the arena to do what needed to be done so the horse would get the proper help at the exact proper moment? (Whew! I did write it again. I hope y'all got it this time if you missed it the first time.) That, my friends, was *FEEL!* That was situational awareness. And that's not a gift that some just have and others do not. It is a skill. A skill that can be developed with practice and hard work.

The key to success is spending one's limited valuable time and one's limited valuable energy working at and practicing the right things. That's what made Tom Dorrance and Ray Hunt such great horsemen of their time. Where others may work to practice more physical skills Mr. Tom, Mr. Ray, Mr. Jack, and others worked hard to practice skills such as situational awareness, the timing of the horse, and how and why the horse did what he did. The development of those skills put them in the right place at the right time to help the horse at the right moment. By helping the horse, they helped themselves. By helping themselves, they helped the horse.

Has the question "What in the hell does 'Reward the thought' mean?" been answered yet? In a way, yes. As I recalled in my mind all that I witnessed while at Mr. Tom's clinic, I thought about his timing and how perfectly well it was developed. What made it "masterful"? What made it masterful was the simplicity of the timing. *The timing.*

I ask my students certain questions so frequently that I'm sure they get sick and tired of me asking. So why do I ask them so frequently? It is of utmost importance they know the answers to certain questions and they know where and when the answers are applicable. One of my favorite questions is, *How do horses learn?* The answer, which you know by now from this book, is: *From the release of pressure.* Period. *How do horses learn? From the release of pressure. How do horses learn? From the release of pressure.* You get my point. *Horses learn from the release of pressure.* Period. This is so incredibly fundamental and important.

A common question that goes with this is, *When do you release?* Ah…a great question. Another great horseman has been quoted as saying, "Reward the slightest try." The word "reward"— what does it refer to? It is what is given to a horse when the horse "tries" to do what you ask him to do. *How do horses learn? From the release of pressure.* Therefore, *the release is the reward.* Let's look now at "try." "Try" in this context is an attempt by the horse to do what we've asked the horse to do. In summary: *How do horses learn? From the release of pressure. The release is the reward. When does one reward the horse? When the horse attempts to do what he's been asked to do.*

So, what does *reward the thought* mean? Simple! Every single physical action we take starts with a thought. Every single physical action a horse takes starts with a thought. Thoughts turn into actions. The split moment in time we detect that a horse is even remotely thinking about what we want him to do is when we should reward—that is, *release pressure.* Do we become mind-readers of the horse? No. of course not. We become extremely situationally aware of the entire body language of the horse. Read the horse. Read the ears, eyes, nostrils, head position, skin, balance on the feet, tail position, rhythm or lack thereof in movement, jaw tension and release of jaw tension. These are all things that are always going on with a horse. There is a line in the movie *Peaceful Warrior* starring Nick Nolte that I refer to a lot and it's very applicable here: "There's never nothing going on."

Learning to read the horse's body language accurately assists us in determining what might be on a horse's mind. We train the horse's mind so the horse can train his body to do what we want him to do. How does one do that? *Reward the thought.*

**This chapter is dedicated to Mr. Tom Dorrance, 1910–2003. I had one other opportunity to work with Mr. Tom. It was during a brief stay at his home a year or so after the clinic. Mr. Jack was right the day he called me. He said it might be Mr. Tom's last clinic in Texas. I learned later it was his last clinic ever. God bless and rest in peace.*

CHAPTER 15

HORSEMANSHIP IS AN OPPORTUNITY TO PRACTICE "HUMANSHIP"

IN THE EARLY 2000s—2003, maybe 2004—I was doing a horsemanship tour with Purina Mills. Part of that tour had me performing horsemanship demonstrations at an agricultural farm show in Mitchell, South Dakota. Mitchell is very much a farming community. It is also the home of the World's Only Corn Palace. Of course, while in Mitchell, I had to go see the Corn Palace. Yup, it was built with corn. Lord knows the area surely produces enough resources to build such a thing. At least every field I saw had corn in it. I suppose to folks raised in the Midwest or other major farm areas, acres and acres of corn fields is a common site. For me, it was not. I'd seen corn fields, lots of them, but until visiting Mitchell, South Dakota, I had no idea what *a lot* of corn was. Heck, even while driving to Mitchell along I-90, I saw nothing but corn fields as far as I could see. Even the farm show was in the middle of a corn field. It looked as if the corn had been cut down and the rows had been leveled just for the event. The perimeter was…you guessed it, corn fields.

I guess you might remember from chapter 5 (p. 42) that Mitchell was where I met one bright young reporter who asked me what my message was. And I guess you know now that my message is that horsemanship is an opportunity to practice "humanship" every day. In my work with people at the ranch, clinics, or expositions like the agricultural farm show in South Dakota, I consistently see the parallel between horsemanship and "humanship." In my opinion, to be successful in both, it's imperative to be aware of what it is one wants, to have timing as to how and when to ask for it, and finally to be well-balanced in one's approach toward obtaining it. In my decades as a professional horseman, I've now worked with thousands of people. I've learned that the most difficult question for them to answer is, *What do you want?* It's a simple question until someone tries to answer it specifically. However, without knowing what you want, how do you start toward obtaining it? Without knowing what you want, how do you know if you get it? Therefore, it's obviously very important to *know what you want* in order to work toward obtaining it or achieving it.

Once it is determined what you want, when does the work begin toward obtaining it or achieving it? The answer highly successful people respond with is, "Now." Timing for less successful individuals might be a bit different. Those folks might respond with, "Tomorrow." The timing might be even more different for yet another group, and their response might be something like, "One of these days," or "When I get around to it."

Let's say for now you've decided what you want, *specifically*. It's been determined you will begin working toward it *now*. Which raises the question, "How?" This is where *balance* comes into play. It's important to have a balanced approach. An approach that's too passive and results may not occur in a timely manner. An approach that is too aggressive may yield less than thorough results or results with too much anxiety attached. Perhaps the goal would be to have an approach that is balanced. Perhaps one's approach could *be as light as possible but as firm as necessary*. These are important concepts in both horsemanship and "humanship." The practice of combining awareness, timing, and balance requires an organized process. One's process must be simply and logically laid out in one's mind. When the thoughts of the process make sense and those thoughts are put into action, the results can be measured.

The reason I say that horsemanship is an opportunity to practice "humanship" is because in order to have consistent measurable success with a horse, one needs to constantly evaluate oneself. There's not a better source of feedback of one's own performance than a horse. Why? Remember what we talked about in chapter five: The horse is one hundred percent honest. He has no ulterior motives for his behavior. He doesn't stress over events of the past nor does he worry about what may or may not happen in the future. He's not holding a grudge because you fed him late last week. He does not dread the farrier appointment next week. Horses live very much in the moment of *now*. Because a horse has no concerns for anything other than what is affecting him *now*, he gives immediate, honest feedback to anything we present to him. If the response you get from the horse is favorable, then whatever you did might have worked. If you did not like the response of the horse, then what you just did might *not* have worked.

In order to get a horse to "follow" us, we must prove to the horse that we mean him no harm. We must build trust, we must be worthy of respect, we must display confidence so the horse will feel confident. To achieve all of these, we must know a little about the horse, and have empathy for him. These are characteristics we want to see in others and in ourselves. These are characteristics horses like to see in us as well. A great way to help develop these characteristics is through horsemanship.

What I like about using horsemanship to teach "humanship" is that in our world of instant gratification, people want to see immediate results. Yet horses, unlike us, live in the moment. They are only concerned about now. They are very keenly aware that they have no control over yesterday or tomorrow. Wouldn't it be cool if we could do that? Quit worrying about what happened yesterday. We have no control over the past. Similarly, we have no control over the future, either. Our actions today may influence what may happen down the road, but there's no controlling it. So, why not, like the horse, be in the now? Why not be in the present? It's a humble thought, but it's all we have. We have the moment we are experiencing now. Horses help us stay focused on all that is taking place in the moment.

For those who crave instant gratification—instant response and instant feedback—well, there's no better source than the horse and there's no better practice than horsemanship.

CHAPTER 16

RIDE EVERY STRIDE

A FEW YEARS ago, I decided to host a podcast. That is, *after* I learned what the heck a podcast was. I'd heard the term but knew little more than there was something out there with that name. In my mind, it was a more modern technical description of a radio program. (I'm reasonably sure I listened to plenty and just thought I was listening to radio programs.) Then, one of my friends, Laura McClellan, educated me a little and encouraged me to consider hosting a podcast of my own. In fact, she was doing one that was growing in popularity with each episode. (The Productive Woman is still wildly successful today.)

I met Laura after she read an article in the popular equestrian magazine *Horse & Rider* that featured me and the success I was having in Versatility Ranch Horse events. (These are insanely popular now, but at the time of the article, Versatility Ranch Horse was new to most people.) Because of the combination of my practical knowledge of ranch work, my experience in training performance horses, and my work ethic, I was having exceptional showings with relatively young horses.

Well, as God and luck would have it, Laura McClellan noticed at the end of the article the writer referenced my location. She showed it to her husband because he was seeking help with a young Palomino filly he had been gifted and our locations, Sulphur Springs and Greenville, were only minutes apart. Laura and her husband Mike arranged to come out to the ranch and discuss their situation with the filly. Little did I know at the time that Laura would become such an inspiration in my life.

First, Laura's story is truly one that would inspire anyone, and especially young women. Second, her journey to become a rider had such a simple goal: to simply feel the wind blow in her hair at a canter…without fear. This goal would challenge me to be a much better teacher, communicator, and motivator. Did the tide ever turn. Laura, with all her achievements, taught me volumes about myself and my skills and the boundaries I had placed on myself on many levels, many of which I still struggle with today, but inspired by her, I've learned to keep moving forward. Laura became a close friend that generally cared about me and the message she felt I must share with others. Through our countless long conversations, she encouraged me to quit simply taking notes and thinking about writing this book and to actually get on with doing it. Laura also inspired this chapter. *Ride Every Stride* is not only the chapter title, it is also the title of my podcast, which she co-hosted for the first seventy or so episodes.

Laura is one of the most accomplished people I know. She came to me because she wanted to fulfill a simple childhood dream of riding a horse again. Because of all the successes she had already experienced in her life, I thought it would be a piece of cake to help her achieve loping around the arena "with the wind blowing in her hair." It seemed to me there was nothing she couldn't do. There was no doubt she'd be good at this horse-riding thing.

The problem was that she had zero confidence. That blew my mind. She had achieved so much in her education, in her professional life, and as a mother. How did she accomplish so much and have so little confidence in herself? I began to question if I was the guy to help her reach her dream of getting on that horse. I didn't know how to motivate her. I didn't know how to help her overcome her fears. She was scared to be within ten feet of a horse in the beginning. I began to realize that Laura favored two words that I absolutely hate: "I can't." I'd tell her she was going to have to get close to this horse, love on him, pet him, brush him, and simply be around him.

"I can't."

"Why can't you?"

"I'm afraid."

If my memory serves me correctly, I shared with her a story about a schoolteacher, Mamie McCullough, aka "The I Can Lady." Miss Mamie wrote an entire curriculum on "I Can." It was so successful that she gained the attention of motivational speaker Zig Ziglar. He asked Miss Mamie to join his organization. That is where I met her. She spoke at a motivational seminar I attended. One of her quotes that got my attention (and laughs from the entire audience) was, "When I hear 'I can't,' what I really hear is either 'I don't know how' or 'I won't.' If you don't know how, let me teach you. If you won't, let me spank you."

Well in Laura's case, I certainly was not going to attempt spanking her. Besides, she was a lawyer at one of the state's oldest and most prestigious law firms. I figured I'd be much better off trying to teach her how to overcome her fear issues. We gradually worked step by step, inch by inch (like we talked about in chapter 3—p. 23) to where we got Laura comfortable around the horses. Eventually she brushed them and braided their manes and tails. The next thing was to teach her to do some groundwork exercises to make her realize that she could be the leader in the horse-human relationship. After all, she was a leader in other relationships. At first, Laura walked the horse with a lead rope and eventually lunged him around her. She did all that very well. And eventually, we got her to sit in the saddle, and later, she started riding a few steps.

I watched as Laura's fears changed. She seemed concerned less and less about being physically harmed by the horse, despite her being quite a small lady and Scooter, the horse I'd selected for her to work with most, was a large horse. The new fear perhaps revealed why she was such an overachiever. She didn't want to try something and not succeed at it. She didn't want to look bad in front of a professional horseman. Please don't think for a moment that Laura was vain. Actually, she was far from it. She was a Type-A personality. She was afraid of being judged and afraid of failing.

During one lesson, Laura was doing quite well, and I have a habit of yelling out, "Good job! That's perfect!" when that is the case. On this day, because she was doing a particularly good job, in my opinion, I was saying it a lot. Suddenly, Laura stopped Scooter in the middle of the exercise and addressed me firmly with, "Oh, damn it! Quit patronizing me. I'm smart enough to know that's *not* perfect!"

Shocked by her mini-outburst, I paused for a moment, sort of grinned, and replied, "That's perfect *for now*. When you get consistent at it, then I'll raise the bar." I truly believe that exchange helped us both.

Fortunately, over the course of several months, Laura not only got over her initial fear of horses, she also learned to manage her concerns about being judged by me, and she dealt with her fear of failing to achieve her goal simply by achieving it. She worked hard and earned each and every improvement until she accomplished what she set out to accomplish. She focused on what she wanted to achieve, which was to be on horseback, loping around the arena. It was a huge learning experience for her and for me. And the true reward? We became close friends.

Frequently, I'm told that Ride Every Stride is great podcast title. I'm also asked regularly why the show is named what it is.

Ride every stride is a phrase I use quite regularly. To me it means to be present, in the moment, and keenly aware of what is happening *right now*. What are we doing with *this* horse, right now? We can't be distracted; we have to be focused every step of the way. Being distracted in any number of situations is potentially dangerous. I think this is especially so when around an animal as big, strong, and fast as a horse. Things can happen very quickly. Good things can happen, but so can things that are not so good. Therefore, it's important to be aware of each moment, perhaps each stride, along the way.

An analogy I often use relates to driving a car. I ask my students or clinic participants, "How many of you drive?" Usually, it's almost all of them. "Would you wait until you hit a fence or power pole before you moved your steering wheel to guide your vehicle back toward the middle of the road? Isn't your plan to stay in your lane? Sure. So, do you wait until you run off the road and hit something before you correct the steering wheel, or are you constantly involved with adjusting and guiding the vehicle so you can eventually reach your destination without incident?"

So, with *ride every stride*, it means we don't wait until the horse runs off into a ditch before we guide him back onto the path. I've heard people say they used to ride horses but got tired of being brushed off under trees or rubbed off by a fence or taken back to the barn (by the horse). They want to blame the horse as if the horse had some ill intent to get the rider off his back. I listen carefully to those complaints, but to be honest, I'm thinking, "Hmmm. How'd he get to the tree? How'd he get close enough to the fence to rub you off? Where were you and what were you doing or *not* doing while the horse was making his own way back to the barn?" Well, to go back to my analogy, your car doesn't suddenly run off the road and hit a power pole. What were you doing or not doing from the time the vehicle left the middle of your lane until it hit the ditch and finally the power pole?

Bottom line: We must be present; we must take accountability and responsibility for our actions or lack of actions. If we're not getting what we want, whose fault is that? We could blame the barn, the tree, the fence, the horse, or all the other things in our life that are a potential distractions. Or, we could simply accept accountability and responsibility for ourselves and guide ourselves back on the path on which we want to stay. *Focus on what you want and where you want to go.* The difference between focusing on what you want or focusing on what you *don't* want is very little. Yet the end result can truly be huge—life-changing, in fact. The truth is, we get in life that on which we focus the most.

As I've talked about in these pages, I trained horses and raised my daughters with this philosophy. I focused on the behavior that I wanted. I set them up to be successful. In other words, I put them on the path to do what I wanted… then I let them be. Every time they got off course, I put them back on course and let them be again. With the girls, I might cautiously sit back and watch to make sure they weren't going to hurt themselves, but I'd allow mistakes to happen and observe their responses. Sometimes they would correct themselves. When they did, I would praise them. When they needed correcting, I simply put them back on course and let them be again. After a while, the safest and best place to be was on course. The best place, the place most comfortable, the happiest place, was on course (remember *the path of least resistance?*). The key was to be present and focused on the desirable path, so to speak.

When working with horses, be present. Be in the moment. Be engaged enough to keep the horse on course or put him back on course. Sometimes, it's about the horse, but most of the time, it's about us. We have to stay focused on what we want. Be consistent and be persistent. Allowing the horse to choose the path of least resistance actually empowers the horse. In time the horse learns to train the rider to quit correcting him. How? By staying on course. Everyone wins. The rider wins because the horse chooses to stay on course. The horse wins because he's not being corrected.

Consider again the four questions I explain on p. 34. By learning these questions and applying them as a guideline to stay focused and stay in the moment, achieving the things you want in life and with your horse becomes more realistic. Remember, the difference between focusing on what you want rather than on what you don't want is…*don't.*

I think about those four questions every stride of the way. It's so much easier to be in the now and focus on what we want when we keep ourselves and our horses on the path of least resistance. *Ride every stride.*

I dedicate this chapter to my inspirational friend Laura McClellan.

CHAPTER 17

LUCK IS WHEN PREPARATION MEETS OPPORTUNITY

In 1992, I bought my facility in Sulphur Springs, Texas. It was a house, a small thirty-six- by forty-eight-foot barn, and perimeter fencing. It was a property I was familiar with already. During my youth the Beasingers, an elderly retired farming couple, lived there in an old run-down farmhouse. It was easy to imagine that at some point the house was beautiful. Because of its size, one could assume the Beasingers were a large family, although no one I knew recalled seeing anyone ever being there other than Mr. and Mrs. Beasinger. My grandparents' land joined the Beasinger place, and from time to time my grandmother would check in on them. When they passed away, my grandfather bought their land. It made sense for him to do so. A few years later, my aunt and uncle bought the property from my grandfather and had the old farmhouse torn down and a new house built a few yards in front of where the old one had stood.

While I was living in New Zealand, I received a phone call from home informing me that my aunt and uncle were divorcing and selling the new house and the land it was built on. I was heartbroken for my aunt's sake but elated for my own young family. At the time, Jazmin, my oldest daughter, was still not one year old. We made all the necessary arrangements to leave New Zealand—I resigned from my job, we sold off all the belongings we had acquired while there, and said goodbye to several friends in the Nelson region that we had grown close to during our stay. I drove our car with tons of luggage to Auckland while my wife and baby Jaz flew there. (We felt it would be quicker and less stressful for both mom and baby.) Our last few days in New Zealand were spent with family and selling our car. Fortunately, everything went without a hitch. And…we moved back to Texas and bought the Beasinger place. Like my grandfather's original acquisition of the property, it just made sense to do so.

There was a lot to do to make the new Hargis place an outfit. Horse-safe fences had to be built around the property. Pens and corrals had to be planned and constructed, as well as stalls inside the small barn. There was much to do. All it would take was time and money. It would be my time, because I had no money to hire help. Whenever I contemplated hiring someone, my grandfather would ask, "Whatcha got more of? Time or money?" Which was his way of telling me to get to work. I knew if I prioritized the building projects correctly, I could keep horses safe while the place was brought up to speed, and it wasn't long before I started getting some horse training business.

About a year later, things were going pretty well. My reputation of being handy with horses began to spread. Eventually a rancher named Marlin Ingram down the way from Quitman, Texas, called. Marlin was an eccentric fella. He was an "Aggie" and both his sons were attending Texas A&M, too. He and his family were very much in the cattle business. They had a good-sized ranch by East Texas standards and specialized in selling breeder bulls and replacement heifers. He'd started dabbling a little in horses and purchased a high-powered Peppy San Badger bred, black-and-white overo paint stallion to put on his mares. Their babies were coming of age to get going under saddle, and he wanted me to do it. There were to be about ten to fifteen colts a year that would need to be started and then marketed for him.

Mr. Ingram loved horses, but you could tell by the horses he raised that he didn't know a lot about handling them. In the beginning of our working relationship, he would often bring me horses to get started under saddle that had not seen a human much at all, or what little interactions they'd had with humans were bad experiences. It wasn't uncommon for him to chase his horses into his corrals with his Ford truck. He'd often run them through chutes like cattle to deworm them and vaccinate them. Like I said, he was a cattle man. In his mind, the chutes were efficient for working cattle, and since horses were livestock, too, then the same practice would do for them. Needless to say, all of these were unpleasant experiences from the horses' perspective. Once at my place, they came around after a while, but getting them to do so was challenging for a young trainer.

Mr. Ingram was a very spiritual and religious man. I appreciated that. Through our relationship with the horses, he began to trust me, and he eventually asked me to come to his ranch and help with both his cattle and the horses.

I could not help but notice that his place was always immaculately kept. His grass was always mowed. The fence rows were clean. It looked like a showplace. The Ingram Ranch was large. For it to be that nicely kept a lot of time and attention had been committed. I couldn't help but think he had a boatload of people working for him whose job was to maintain it all. I asked him one day how many people worked for him. He said he had no employees. The ranch was kept up strictly by him and Marlene, his wife, and his two boys who came home from college during school breaks and summer to help. He said they did it all.

"We get up when the rooster crows," he said. "We work until everything we want done gets done."

I told him how impressed I was that they all worked so hard to keep the place in such great shape. We were riding in the cab of his old ranch truck when I said that to him. He didn't respond. In fact, it got eerily quiet in the truck. I could hear every sound the vehicle made as we rattled and bumped down the poorly maintained county road. Then I thought I heard a bit of a sniffle. I turned and looked over at Mr. Ingram. He was teary-eyed. I apologized to him for touching a nerve. I hadn't meant to upset or offend him. Although I didn't understand how my compliment would be upsetting or offensive.

He said, "Oh, no. You didn't offend me. I just thought about how whenever I go to the barber shop or the farmers' co-op in town, all those boys tell me how lucky I am."

I didn't really understand how that would make him emotional about what I'd said, so I asked if he'd explain.

"Well, the other day I went to the barber shop," he went on. "As soon as I walked in, the barber said, 'There's Lucky Marlin.'" The barber and the men in the shop chuckled and went on about him being lucky. Each time he'd go to town, the folks would joke about his luck: "The luckiest man in Quitman, Texas." "The luckiest man in Wood County." He claimed that when he'd ask why they all thought he was lucky, they'd say he was lucky to have such a pretty wife. Lucky to have such a nice well-kept property. Lucky to have such quality cattle. Lucky to have such good horses. They credited everything he had worked hard for to luck. They didn't consider the countless hours of hard work put in to making the place all that it appeared to be. "It didn't get beautiful on its own," he said.

I was still trying to grasp why he was so emotional when he went on.

"I got to thinking about what the barber and all the others say. Rather than being offended by them thinking I was lucky to have such a beautiful place, I wanted to think differently about 'luck.' The luck is actually them driving by and seeing it look so good. The luck is when somebody comes to buy one of my bulls and sees how clean my place is and then I can ask top dollar for that bull. I guess luck is self-made. I guess the boys in town taught me a lesson. They taught me that *I am* a very lucky man. I realized the meaning of luck is when preparation meets opportunity. The opportunity to clean and maintain this place occurs every day. Marlene and I get out here and weed-eat, cut grass, trim trees, and fix fence. We don't let a day go by without taking the opportunity to pick up, clean, or do something productive. As a result, when a customer comes, I'm prepared. I'm prepared to ask top dollar. My place is clean; my cattle are healthy. It all ties in together."

Luck is when preparation meets opportunity. That hit a spot with me. Perhaps there is no such thing as luck. Perhaps luck is what we make it. If luck is indeed when preparation and opportunity meet, then we all have the opportunity to prepare in one way or another throughout our waking hours. We each have an opportunity to make our own luck every day. By preparing, one can be ready for whatever opportunity arises.

I'm not a gambler by any stretch of the imagination, but I've noticed over the last decade or so an increased interest in poker. It's even televised. I was raised to think that gambling was about luck or the lack of it. Yet, when you listen to the professional poker players, they'll tell you it's not about luck; don't "gamble." It's about knowing your opponent, knowing the cards, knowing the odds, and knowing the game that you're playing. Never sit down at a table depending on luck. The "luck" good players have is what they create by knowing the game, knowing their opponent, knowing human nature. Every chance they get, they study the game itself, study people, study human habits, even study themselves. They use preparation and opportunity to make their own luck.

This reminds me of a time when my wife and I were asked to join friends on a trip to a modest Louisiana casino. I had never been to a casino and was curious, so we agreed to go. I was particularly interested in watching the craps table. A rancher I rode horses for and did a lot of cattle work for went to the National Finals Rodeo in Las Vegas every year. Every year he'd win enough money at the craps table to pay for the entire trip for both himself and his wife. I'd often say that he must be lucky, and he'd quickly respond back that luck had nothing to do with it. He'd also say he never gambled. To me it all sounded contradictory. I wondered, *How can you gamble without gambling and how can you win at gambling without luck?*

Because of my perception on luck and gambling, I didn't test my luck and I didn't gamble. However, Mr. Hurley's stories about Vegas and winning each year at the craps table intrigued me. So, as soon as my wife and I arrived at the casino, I made my way to one of the many craps tables. At first I was not interested in playing. I simply wanted to observe…prepare. Well, let me tell you, I was overwhelmed. I couldn't begin to understand all the goings on at the table. It seemed like madness. People were talking loudly, yelling things I didn't understand, rolling dice, tossing chips, sliding chips, exchanging money for chips. All this was happening on a table with more numbers and colors than a country boy could shake a stick at. To me, it all seemed like luck…bad luck. I saw a lot more people losing money than winning money. This did not seem like a game for me. Then, my wife and I noticed one man at the table that was much quieter than the others. He also had stacks and stacks of casino chips. He won at least a few chips each time someone rolled the dice. Occasionally he'd win a lot of chips when someone rolled the dice. I said to my wife, "*That's* the guy we need to watch." So I watched him. I tried to figure out what he did and why he did it. I began to understand at least a little, but I was still as lost as a ball in high weeds.

Finally, the man asked me if I was going to play.

"No sir," I replied. "Too complicated for me, but obviously you've got it figured out."

He said he was just a student of the game. When I referred to his huge stack of chips (which, by the way, were perfectly organized by color in the built-in spaces on the table), he glanced at them matter-of-factly and mentioned if I was interested in learning to play, he'd help me. Then he said, "I'll give you your first lesson. The most important one…" He paused. "Don't gamble." Again, I referenced his stack of chips. "You don't win that by gambling, and you don't win it quickly," was his reply.

I remembered my grandfather's words: *Whatcha got more of? Time or money?* I also recalled another quote about patience that you all know now, too: *Everything comes to he who waits…so long as he who waits works like hell while he waits.* I'd learned about patience. I had time; we were going to be in Louisiana a couple of days. I was going to work to learn a little about this game.

Because of a few tips and strategies the professional "gambler" taught me at the casino in southern Louisiana, my wife and I can now usually fund trips to Vegas or other casinos with the chips I win at the craps table. Again, I'm not a gambler by any stretch. I simply combine the information I was taught with strict discipline and endless patience to win. Perhaps the perception of others is that I'm lucky.

I think "luck" is applicable in almost every situation. I've been blessed to have started well over a thousand head of horses during my career as a professional horseman. The more I learn and the harder I work, the luckier I get. I can count on both hands how many times I've had young horses buck with me over the last twenty years of my near five-decade career. In fact, I think I've failed myself and failed the horse if a horse feels the need to buck with me in the saddle. On more than one occasion I've heard people say after watching me start a colt, "It's lucky he didn't buck." There was a time in my career when that statement would have offended me. However, now I don't disagree with them. Instead, I chuckle under my breath and think about Mr. Marlin Ingram and the countless hours I've worked and prepared. I think of how grateful I am for all the opportunities folks have given me to start their colts under saddle. I think, *Yep, preparation meets opportunity.*

Good luck or bad luck is not something to do with fate. In my opinion, it is something to do with faith. I have no doubt in my mind that luck is created by the practice of good sound principles of success, regardless of where those principles are applied. When applied to business, you might be the lucky one whose investment pays off. When applied to fishing, you might be the one who catches the limit. When applied to sports, you might be the one who gets the score. When applied to your ranch, you might be the one with the beautiful livestock and profitable property. When applied to craps, you might be the one with all the chips. When applied to horsemanship, you might be the one with the really nice horse.

Earlier in this book I said I was blessed to have lived a hard life. I'm certain that the challenges of my youth and throughout my career have taught me to appreciate the value of sound principles. Principles such as foresight, initiative, work ethic, discipline, courage, and empathy are instrumental in succeeding in any number of areas in one's life. Developing and practicing solid principles surely prepares us for the countless opportunities presented to us along our life's journey.

In that I wish you the best of "luck."

CHAPTER 18

BLOOM LIKE A ROSE

By the middle of my junior year in high school, it was becoming apparent that my goal of playing college football would be realized. I began to take more seriously the courses that would better prepare me to be a college student. One course, in particular, that I desperately needed was taught by a popular but demanding teacher, Mrs. Janet Peek. The course was Advanced Senior English, and it was a challenging class that prepared us for ACT and SAT tests, as well as college-level English courses.

Prior to taking Mrs. Peek's English course, I had little confidence in my ability to express my thoughts in writing. Somehow, Mrs. Peek seemed to find something in each of her students that she could use to inspire and motivate us. With me, for example, she used her experiences with previous student athletes, and of course her own son, Chris. Chris graduated a couple of years before me and had been quite the high school athlete. Like me, he was a four-sport letterman. Also like me, he aspired to play football at a higher level. Mrs. Peek knew and appreciated the way young men could think about and stress over balancing sports and academics. She used this knowledge and her own insightful ways to encourage others and me to practice written communication skills.

Two assignments in Advanced Senior English made up significant portions of our final grade. One was a research paper and the other a long essay or short story. Our research paper topics were chosen from the current events of the time. The topics were chosen by Mrs. Peek, carefully written on a small square of paper, thoughtfully folded, then dropped in a large-mouthed, empty plastic condiments jar from our school cafeteria. With mischievous delight Mrs. Peek shook the jar, thoroughly mixing and tossing the folded papers about as she walked up and back among the desks in her classroom. One by one, each senior in the class drew a research paper topic from the jar. We were instructed not to unfold the paper until she told us to. We waited. No one broke Mrs. Peek's rules. She was fun and fair, but we all respected the fact that she was firm.

After each drawing she'd shake the large jar again. Predictably, with only one last piece of paper remaining in the jar, she shook it. The anticipation was part of the fun, and Mrs. Peek knew it. She enjoyed making us wait. Finally, she gave us permission to look. Our fingertips went to work frantically opening the meticulously folded mini-squares of paper. Some of the students groaned when reading their assignment topics. Some cheered. Thankfully, I cheered. My topic just happened to be the world's most-talked-about current event of the time: the upcoming wedding of Prince Charles and Lady Diana Spencer. Needless to say, I would have no trouble finding material to support my paper.

On both the research paper and short story or essay assignments (I chose to write an essay), I surprised even myself as to the effort I put in. The research paper was due first and I made an "A" on it. A couple weeks later, our short stories or essays were due. Once the projects had been reviewed, Mrs. Peek announced that one student had written a publish-worthy essay. At first she spoke vaguely about the writing, the choice of topic, and so on. As she continued, I began thinking that some of what she was saying was very relevant to my work. Then I realized she was referring to my work. *I was the student she was referring to.* She began reading my essay aloud to the class. I sank in my chair with fear that my work would not be appreciated by my classmates. Then I began to notice that the class was sitting on the edge of their seats and listening to every word Mrs. Peek read. My emotions were torn between pride and embarrassment.

At the end of the reading Mrs. Peek asked the author of the paper to stand. The class was shocked that Mr. CHS "Joe Jock" athlete Van Hargis was the writer of the publish-worthy piece.

What Mrs. Peek said next has been a part of who I am to this day: "Mr.

Hargis, stand. Be proud of your growth. I want you to bloom…bloom like a rose."

No one I went to school with knew much about my upbringing. Most knew the apparent things, such as my mother and I were not of the upper class in our community. My mother and stepfather were divorced. I was a jock and an average student. Some may have known where my mother worked and that she at times had more than one job. We were not secretive. I think we simply got good at hiding our hurt and pain. In a way I think we were ashamed of it. I know I was. We didn't talk about it to anyone other than our immediate family—more specifically, my grandparents. So, when Mrs. Peek chose those words, "Bloom like a rose," to encourage me, she hit a nerve deep inside my soul. If a kid could go from being beaten, abused, discouraged, manipulated, and made fun of and still have the potential to grow, develop, and one day "bloom" and be encouraged to do so, then perhaps it was true that we can all rise above our past and achieve whatever it is we choose to do.

> Life is a grand thing indeed.
> We strive toward goals, to succeed.
> Whatever we choose to do in life
> win or lose,
> it's what we do along the way
> that makes us who we are today.
>
> —VH

I appreciated the fact Mrs. Peek was well-respected among the students and among her peers. Looking back, I knew right away those words she spoke that day meant something to me. However, at the time, I didn't realize how impactful they would be or that they'd stay with me throughout my life. Perhaps, somehow, Mrs. Peek did. As a matter of fact, when Mrs. Peek signed my high school yearbook in the Spring of 1981, she wrote some encouraging words in big, bold letters and quotation marks: *Remember, Bloom Like a Rose.* I'm so grateful for those words. She saw potential in me and wanted me to be multi-dimensional. She encouraged it.

I'm certain that part of God's plan is to insert the right people in our lives at the right time. The timing with Mrs. Peek was perfect.

At some point during the years following high school, I had somewhat constrained the full meaning of the words *bloom like a rose*. I had limited the words to be somewhat synonymous with "potential." Then, an experience with one of my college football coaches planted another seed of thought in my mind.

I had just scored a touchdown and was obviously quite pleased with myself. This was demonstrated by the typical post-touchdown celebratory excitement. I finally made my way over to the sidelines, and amongst all the butt pats, high fives, and helmet slaps was Coach Crawford's voice saying in his characteristics gruff tone, "Good job, Hargis. Anyone ever tell you that you've got potential?"

"Yes, sir!" I answered, still excited.

"Well, that just means you ain't done nothin' yet," he quipped as he walked away.

In other words, what I did in that game was good. But it was my job. I was a running back, for goodness sake. My job was to get the ball, run north and south, and try like hell to get in the end zone. I did that. During all my years of football, I did that a lot. I was doing what was expected of me. Is that really fulfilling one's potential?

Wait a minute…if my potential here is in question, then what the heck did *bloom like a rose* really mean?

For years I scratched my head on this conundrum. Again, as God would have it, a horsemanship clinic with my hero and mentor Mr. Jack Brainard would enlighten me a bit. You'll remember that he, too, said something that struck a nerve in my soul. He said something that connected a few dots for me. *I'm just afraid I'm going to die before I learn everything I want to learn about these darned horses.* Mr. Jack was one of the most knowledgeable and respected horsemen of our time. For him to make such a statement made me realize we never stop learning. We never stop growing. We should *never* reach our potential. When we do, we are done.

Perhaps to *bloom like a rose* means something a little different to me now. At some point in your life you will be a seed. Someone will love you, nurture you, and work to develop you. You will begin to grow, perhaps somewhat on your own. There will be good weather and there will be bad. Those that love and care for you may prune away the dying parts of you and perhaps prop up your stems. Eventually a bud will begin to appear and give those around you hope in your development. Soon, the bud begins to open and others anticipate the more that will come. Then the hope turns to reality when the flower of the rose is fully open and beautiful. The beauty is shared with all to see and enjoy. Nectar, pollen, aroma, and the beautiful sight of a flower fully developed. Oh, so beautiful.

The beauty is short-lived though. Colors begin to fade, the nectar begins to dry, the pollen is dispersed, and the petals begin to fall. But those who know and love the rose know it will begin again the process of nurturing, growth, and development—and a bud will once again appear, along with the hope and anticipation that the bud will bloom again.

I saw Mrs. Peek not long ago, and she's just as energetic and enthusiastic as she always was. I hugged her and she patted me on the back. We reminisced a bit and with tears I said, "Thank you for encouraging me to bloom like a rose, Mrs. Peek."

In my life's journey I have been blessed to have discovered my spiritual gift so that my growth as a human and a horseman may help others find theirs. I am grateful that so many people and animals have helped me in countless ways grow, develop, and bloom, again and again. I've learned that in horsemanship and in "humanship," the journey is never-ending. Like the rose, we will produce, and give joy and purpose to others over and over until there is no more life in our stems. It is then and only then that our walk on earth is done.

I sincerely pray you have no desire to retire
and that you will forever...

...bloom like a rose.

**I dedicate this chapter to Mrs. Janet Peek. Her encouraging words animatedly spoken to me in her classic and enthusiastic style during my transition years into adulthood reminded me to try and challenged me to do that which I may not have done without knowing someone cared. If, in fact, I did "bloom like a rose," it was because the Janet Peeks of the world pruned me, groomed me, and had faith in me... despite my thorns.*